A NEW START ®

A Guide to
Starting Your Own Business

Cassius. V. Stuart

First Edition
International Standard Book Number: 978-0-578-49197-4 Printed in USA
Written by Cassius V. Stuart | www.BluSkiesSolutions.com
Cover design © 2019 Blu Skies Solutions.
Formatting by Eli Blyden | www.CrunchTimeGraphics.com

AR360 © Copyright Blu Skies Solutions
Download AR360 from Apple Store & Google Play

App Store   Google Play

Dedication

This book is dedicated to the many people who made a difference: my beloved grandfather, Rupert B. Stuart, who passed away March 2, 2003. Daddy, you have been my pillar of strength and my source of encouragement over the years. It is because of you I can write this book. May you rest in peace.

To my beloved wife *Dr. Sharmaine* Stuart, you are the wind beneath my wings. Thank you for your continual love and support. I love you very much! ***To my amazing daughters,*** Syiera, Kayley, Cassidy and Raquell: you all are an inspiration and a joy. You give me the strength and the will to continue to move forward. I love all of you.

My Mother, Ida Stuart, who **supported me 1000%over the years. I love you and many thanks.** To my father Clyde Ifill, thanks for your love and support. I love you. To my good friend who died June 16th, 2003, you are truly missed.

Acknowledgements

To the many people, especially my family members, who have been a positive influence in my life over the years, I say, many thanks.

Special thanks to the late Dr. Myles Munroe and Dr. Richard Pinder. These men have helped to mold me into the man that I am today. I will be forever grateful for the guidance and support they gave me over the years.

To Les Brown, whose encouraging words over the year have been a source of strength and direction.

Table of Contents

Foreword

The environment has never been more accommodating for people with business ideas to convert them to reality! Almost the entire world is an open market space, accessible to anyone able to convincingly sell a new, improved, or repackaged product or service.

Investors in new business ventures know that most of such efforts fail. While the degree of success for business start-ups varies from one environment to another, depending on many factors (mostly related to support available to the entrepreneur), there is one factor which is always a heavy determinant in new business success. This is the degree to which the person going into business understands how to establish and how to manage such an undertaking. As Cassius Stuart points out so well in this book, starting a business, if it is to be more than just a start, requires preparation.

A NEW START is an entirely current, practical and comprehensive road-map to setting up and managing a new business. It provides guidance on every essential aspect of this often-complex process and would be an essential resource not only to the business novice, but also to the small and medium-sized business which may need to be more fully structured itself to succeed.

I am honored to have been invited to introduce the book to you, and strongly recommend it to those who wish to be successful in business.

– Julian W. Francis, CBE Former Governor of The Central Bank of The Bahamas

> **The last remaining sustainable competitive advantage... is the capacity to learn.**
>
> — Pearlson, K. E., & Saunders, C.

CHAPTER 1

Getting Started

Before we begin the practical application in this book, there are a few questions every potential business owner must address.

1. Why are you going into business?
2. What business will you seek to get in?
3. Will your business offer a product or service?
4. Do you have access to financing?
5. How much money do you think you need to start?
6. When would you like to start your business?
7. Where will your business be located?
8. Do you have business partners?
9. Are you willing to do what it takes to succeed?

As a potential business owner, you should have a clear objective and purpose in mind when deciding to start a business. Before you start your business, you should decide on the type of business you are getting into: will your business be a product or service-based business?

Many small business owners venture into their own business because they think they have a million-dollar idea. They do this without having any experience in basic business procedures nor understand the principles of a successful business. As a result, many start-up businesses fail within the first three years of operation. If a business is to be successful, planning is critical at every stage, particularly in the beginning. Planning is the deciding factor as to whether a business succeeds or fails. Every successful entrepreneur understands this one principle: "If you don't plan, you will fail."

Small business owners should not make the mistake of thinking that because you can produce the product or service and have enough financial support, you can also run a business successfully.

Running a successful business takes skill, hard work and many long hours. If you are not willing to make this sacrifice in your life, then I advise you not to attempt to start your own business. A regular routine job may be best suited for you.

Writing a plan for your business assists you in remaining focused and helps you avoid present and future problems. A business plan is like a detailed map, it shows where a company is going, and how it intends to get there. It also provides knowledge of your destination and how to get there, with very little waste.

Most people, when planning for a major event in their life (for example a holiday or a wedding) develop "somewhat" of a plan. Most of the plan remains in their head, and occasionally they write some points down to help them remember specific details. However, a business plan should be much more formal than simply 'jotting down notes.' It should be used for setting short and long-term goals for your company. It acts as a gauge for evaluating the performance of your company and a barometer to alert you regarding whether or not the business is on the right track.

When planning your business, it is important to set realistic goals. Many business owners hope their businesses become multi-million-dollar operations, but the reality of business is that you must start from the bottom and work your way up to the top. Don't seek to hire 10 employees when you can only afford 3. Don't try to borrow more money than you can realistically repay. Remember, "the journey of a thousand miles always begins with the first step." Start small and watch your business grow!

Why Do I Need
A Business Plan?

A business plan's primary purpose is for procuring start-up capital from potential investors, bankers and other lending institutions. A good business plan will clearly communicate both the strengths and weaknesses of your business.

Businesses around the world have tried to exist without a business plan, only to find failure in the end. A good and detailed business plan is the blue print for a successful business. It also serves as a yardstick for businesses to measure their progress.

Before you can build a house in many countries, by law you need to consult with an architect for a plan (blueprint) of the house you desire. These plans provide you with fore-knowledge on how the house will look and all the details that go along with it; in other words, the finished product.

A plan for a business is no different. You need to have knowledge of how your business will look structurally and financially before you begin. Preparation of a business plan takes time and requires careful consideration of a variety of market and industry factors.

Research must be done about market segments, target markets, location, distribution, competition pricing and so on. All these aspects about your business are like doors and windows drawn on a house plan. A business plan does not guarantee a successful business, but it provides a guide in the right direction. It is a compass in the desert of unemployment and a lighthouse to those who are frustrated with a regular 9-to-5 job. Other factors that are critical to the success of a new business are personnel, management, location, timing, and financial leverage. These factors may ultimately determine the success or failure of a new business.

A solid business plan provides a sense of security to venture capitalists and other lending institutions. It is an important working document and a financial guide which incorporates a "strategic plan" from which the business is operated over time.

A good business plan is a well put together, well thought-out document that gives entrepreneurs the tools they need to make sound business decisions. However, be mindful that it also requires time and comprehensive research. A business plan is never a finished document, but a living document that is always in progress. Most business plans will need to be updated and adjusted based on unforeseen markets or governmental changes. If your business plan is done, so is your business. A good business plan should grow with your business and should be dynamic in its makeup.

It is advisable to have professional assistance in putting your plan together to ensure that you cover all the important details that must be considered. Your chances of success will also increase greatly if you meet with your financial advisor every month.

To reduce the chances of failure, make sure that your business plan is thorough, accurate, and substantive and that the information is all factual. Stay away from trying to make up information because it will only hurt your business in the long run. When generating your financial information, it is critical that you remain as accurate and concise as possible. If you build your business on false data, particularly financial data, you will be destined for failure at the end of the day.

The Entrepreneur

Entrepreneurship is not a new concept. The term entrepreneur has been around for a very long time. An entrepreneur is not just someone who starts and operates a business, but someone who takes the risk and seeks profitable opportunities and takes the necessary steps to accomplish it. Entrepreneurs are trailblazers, pacesetters and pioneers; they are risk-takers and innovators, those who have the courage to do what everyone else is afraid to do. Entrepreneurs are the people that have built our world as we know it today. The many inventions and products that have enhanced the quality of our lives today all came about by someone who dared to use their entrepreneurial spirit.

Regrettably, not all entrepreneurs have an understanding and appreciation for the value of effective planning. In fact, some entrepreneurs feel they can exist without planning. A smart entrepreneur is someone who not only takes risks but measures his risks carefully. He or she understands that making good business decisions requires careful research and planning. A wise entrepreneur knows that good business decisions are made with the availability of information. Information comes from research. Both components together make up the ingredients of a good business plan.

Great entrepreneurs appreciate that to be successful in business, one must understand one of the greatest principles of business: solving problems. In fact, it has been said that the greater the problem solving, the greater the business returns. The Big Four technology companies (**Amazon, Facebook, Google and Apple**) provide solutions to a generation that no other generation before ever imagine.

Amazon is an amazing example of a company which solved a billion-dollar problem. It has become the pioneer and world leader in e-commerce and cloud computing. It brings buyers and sellers together in an e-commerce marketplace. Amazon began as an online book store offering a new way to purchase books, whether digital or print copy. Individuals are now able to by-pass the brick and mortar stores such as Barnes & Noble and purchase books from the comfort of their homes. This new business concept revolutionized the book market and put Jeff Bezos on a path to potentially becoming the richest man in the world. Today, Amazon is the most valuable public company in the world and the largest internet company by revenue.

Facebook is another example of a company that solved a billion-dollar problem. Started in the dormitory of Harvard University by Mark Zuckerberg and a few other college students, Facebook provides a platform to connect people from all over the globe on one social platform. It has evolved from a few Ivy league college students as users in 2004 to over 2.2 billion active users world-wide today.   Facebook has made the world more interconnected than ever before. No matter where you are on the planet, once you have an internet connection you can get connected to Facebook and reach people from all over the globe.

Google created one of the world's most powerful search engines. Google's platform uses an amazing algorithm which gives its users the ability to search and find answers to just about any question. Google was founded by two college students, Larry Page and Sergeyt Brin, who wanted to solve the universal problem of not having access to information on demand. Today, because of its success, the word Google has become synonymous with the word "search." "Google It!" Today, Google has become the world's most valuable brand which now stands at $109.5b (Cox 2017).

Apple is also an astonishing success story. It was created by young and passionate entrepreneurs who wanted to make personal computers available to every home in America and the world. At the time of its inception, computers were huge and were only in large companies or in universities. Steve Jobs, Steve Wozniak and Ronald Wayne had a dream of solving this problem by making computers smaller and more "user friendly". Today, Apple is the first public company to be valued at US$1 trillion with an annual revenue of $256 billion.

While all these companies commenced with a single offering and solving one set of problems, they quickly diversified to provide multiple offerings which afford solutions to billions of people all over the world. Now, Apple produces more than just computers—they make hand-held smartphones, tablet PCs, and wearable technology like watches and fitness trackers. Apple also uses its own operating system-iOS.

What problems exist in the world today which needs solving? Who will provide the next solutions for the next generation? Just as these pioneers studied their times and provided a solution to a problem that was facing their generation, you can do the same. Will the next great idea come from you? As an entrepreneur, don't think that your idea is too small or trivial. You never know how big your idea will grow if you don't "plant the seed."

Think carefully about your idea. It could be the next billion-dollar hit. Just consider 15 years ago, there was no such thing as a smart phone or even an app. Today, about 2.5 billion people have a smart phone. As a result of the smart phone revolution, the app industry exploded. Such revolutionary ideas opened the doors for new jobs and created opportunities for a new, younger and more dynamic kind of entrepreneur.

In such a short span of time, the app industry took over the film and music industry and is projected to balloon to $189 billion by 2020. This new industry provides a bounty of opportunity for those who dare to seize them. What will be the next big app, and will it come from you?

Consider the deficiencies in developing countries. What technological solution can you provide them with to improve their lives? There are many opportunities waiting for you to take advantage of them. You just have to move.

Characteristics Of An Entrepreneur

Entrepreneurs possess many characteristics which ensures their success in business. The characteristics that are most notable in the daily life of an entrepreneur are:

- Great imagination
- Rest
- Action-taking
- Risk-taking
- Failure
- Determination
- Talent
- Need to Achieve
- Self-Confidence and Optimism

Great Imagination

The ability to use your mind's eye is called imagination. This is a powerful tool that gives foresight and ideas to those who may keep doing the same things repeatedly. Imagination is the construction in your mind of images which do not exist in the physical context. It is creating a "virtual reality" in your mind. In other words, you are taking an idea and constructing it all in your mind before anyone even sees it. Successful entrepreneurs see opportunities that others don't; they have great imaginations.

Thomas Edison, one of the greatest inventors and entrepreneurs of the 20th century, had a unique ability to see with his mind's eye. He saw a light bulb when others only saw a lantern. He introduced the first talking moving pictures in 1913 and in all, he patented more than 1,000 discoveries. He was truly a man who used his imagination and profoundly affected the world.

If you want to become a successful entrepreneur, you must learn to develop the ability to use your imagination to see opportunity when others only see obstacles. Remember, everything that exists, exists only because someone had an idea because they were willing to use their imagination.

Rest

One of the secrets to developing a great imagination is rest. Yes, I said rest. Most entrepreneurs believe that they have to push themselves 24/7 to be successful. While I understand the importance of putting major time into your business, it is also imperative to take time to rest.

Resting is so important for us as humans that God made it a command. My personal belief is that if God didn't make it a commandment, we would work and work until our bodies stopped functioning. If you keep pushing yourself as an entrepreneur without resting, your body will not have the time it needs to rebuild needed cells for your optimal function. Resting gives your body time to rejuvenate and stimulate brain function, which is the center of your imagination.

The Jewish nation had it right for centuries, to make rest one of the cornerstones of society. In fact, studies have now proven that individuals who rest get more done and are more productive in their day to day functions.

It is important as an entrepreneur to take some time to rest and to think. Thinking is the main formula for generating new ideas and new dreams.

Action-Taking

Entrepreneurs are action-oriented individuals! To move past your imagination, you need to act. Many people sit and dream of accomplishing grand things, but few stay awake and make it happen. If you want to start your own business or even be successful at anything in life you must be willing to do something. Start to plan where you want to go.

Act and begin to jot down some plans for the direction of your business: what, where, how, when, and why? The fact that you are reading this book is a step in the right direction. Contact the necessary government agencies for business license applications. Talk to a lawyer about the necessary procedures for incorporation.

Now maximize the use of this book and begin to write your business plan. Some plans are more detailed than others. As a result, you may require professional assistance from a business plan consultant. The first step in the right direction is to begin to move, act, and begin to work on your dreams to make them a reality.

Risk-Taking

"The greatest risk in life is not taking one!" To become a successful entrepreneur, you must be willing to take risks. Most people don't realize it, but risks are a part of everyday life. In the business world, however, a smart businessman doesn't just take

any kind of risk, they take calculated risks. Calculated risk is when you understand all the parameters and consequences of your decision before making it. Calculated risks keep you safe during your business life. To discover new oceans, you must first have the courage to leave the shores. You must believe in yourself and your ability and take the risk, knowing that kites rise against the wind rather than with it. If you look at the 10 richest men in the world and consider their success stories you would discover that they too were faced with this step. This step is the determining factor in whether they succeeded or fail.

Risk-taking is the hinge on which the door of success swings. You can't climb a mountain unless you consider and accept the risk of falling. You can't swim the Gulf Stream unless you take the risk of drowning. Finally, you cannot succeed in business unless you face the risk of failing. Risk- taking entrepreneurs are not afraid of failing; in fact, they embrace it. However, failure is not an option in their business ventures. Always remember don't be afraid of failing. Failure is like an x-ray. It allows you to see your mistakes clearly so that you will not make them again. It also allows you to see what the people around you are made of. Don't be afraid to fail in business. Failure is a part of the risk you take. As an entrepreneur, some degree of failure should be anticipated but one should never get comfortable with it. Just keep on trying.

Determination

"If you want anything in life you must be determined enough to fight for it!" Determination is that characteristic that keeps you going despite the odds. Determination is the fuel in the engine of successful entrepreneurs. To get from one point to another, there must be a certain level of risk to begin, but determination will carry you to the end of the journey.

Earlier we spoke about Thomas Edison and his ability to see with his mind's eye. However, consider all those ideas that would have died with him if he did not have the determination to make his ideas into reality. It took Thomas Edison 1,500 times until he was successful in creating the light bulb. This man was so determined to get it right, it didn't matter how many times he failed. Eventually, he did succeed and now the entire planet is benefiting from his determination.

If you want to be successful in your business, you must be determined to go the extra mile. Do a little more and work a little harder. Remember, the race is not to the swift, but to those who are determined to fight until the end. Don't ever, ever give up!

Talent

Talent is an inherent, natural ability to do a thing. Many people have great imaginations. Some are action-oriented, and others are risk-t a k e r s. But if they lack talent, they are like a locked door without a key. Talent is that thing that you are naturally good at. It is perhaps related to your purpose in life.

Consider Michael Jackson, he was a talented musician and entertainer who was born to sing. Singing was his life; however, talent needs to be nurtured and developed. Michael, even though he was born to sing, spent most, if not all his childhood developing this gift (talent). Because of his sacrifice and dedication to develop his talent, the world called him the *king of pop music.*

Michael Jordan is another great example, born to play the game of basketball. He had to develop his gift (talent), practicing hour after hour on his game, defying all odds. Now, he is considered the greatest player to ever play the game of basketball. These individuals are successful at what they do because they enjoy what they do and took the time to develop and nurture their talents; and at the same time, they are doing what they are good at. Like the proverb says, *"Your Gift (talent) makes room for you."*

What talent do you possess? What are you naturally good at? Are you good at painting? It can become a successful business. Are you good at singing? That, too, can become a business. What about public speaking? That, too, can be a lucrative business. Whatever you are good at can become a business if you take the time to develop it.

If you have a talent and passion for app development, video games and gaming, or if you excel in web design or software development—whether Android, .Net, PHP, or Swift =, then you can even hone that talent as well. Such talents can be enhanced by practicing with online protocols and attending workshops or classes which specialize in those types of work. Nearly anything anyone can do, that they excel in, can be considered a talent. One thing talented people do—they practice continuously. Don't work until you get it right. Work at it until there's no way you can get it wrong.

It was only in 2007 that Apple launched its first iPhone. Since then, a new industry was born: the app industry. This new industry created many sub industries such as the gaming industry. These new industries are driven by a new kind of entrepreneur-- an entrepreneur that is not bound by the traditional modus operandi but challenging the status quo and pushing the envelope for new, innovative products and services.

In fact, the gaming industry, with its projected growth to $144 billion by 2020 (Wibowo 2017), has surpassed the music and film industry in both revenue and job creation and from all indications, this market is far from saturation. Since the end of 2016, only 46% of the world's population owns a smart phone (Golmack 2017).

As an entrepreneur, it would be wise to consider looking at the possibilities and future growth of this industry as a potential business venture. This industry gives you a wide range of entry points: from gaming, to products and services, to augmented reality. There are many aspects one can tap into when it comes to the app industry, so it is advisable to take a really good look at this market.

Need To Achieve

The need to achieve is the intrinsic drive hidden in all humans to accomplish a specific goal. This characteristic is the part of the human makeup that makes us uncomfortable with where we are and propels us to excel beyond these limitations. To be a successful entrepreneur, one must not only possess this characteristic but activate it. The need to achieve is the hammer that will break down the wall of mediocrity in your life. It is the wind that enables great men and women to soar to extraordinary heights. Without such a desire, no success is realized, and no accomplishment is attained. The need to achieve is that special something inside that pushes you to go the extra mile. It is that thing that causes you to get up every time you fail. It is that one more try.

Self-Confidence and Optimism

"Believing in yourself, when others don't, is called self-confidence!" Self-confidence is knowing the secret of your inner ability. This secret, most of the time, is not known to people around you and therefore causes them to doubt your ability. Often individuals are not even sure of their own abilities and strengths, which eventually leads to self-doubt and a lack of self-confidence.

Great entrepreneurs possess a certain degree of self-confidence because believing in yourself is the first step in accomplishing your dream. If you want others to believe in you, you must first believe in yourself.

Optimism is the other variable in this equation. It is the ability to keep your head high in the face of disappointment. It is the way one smiles at temporary defeat and keeps moving. Many business owners face tough times in their first three years in operation, but the factor that determines success from failure is the ability to look failure in the face and keep moving. It is the ability to see every obstacle as an opportunity, to see every stumbling block as a stepping-stone, and the ability to use every failure as a learning experience.

Optimism is a characteristic that is essential for successful business owners. It is the ability to *tolerate* failure but not *accept* it. Not every business will succeed. One must face that fact; however, failing in business does not mean you are a failure. Only you can make you a failure.

The great Napoleon, in one of his great campaigns for Italy, did not focus on the Alps (the great mountains), which lay before him, but focused on his objective behind the mountain: Italy. The Alps were just another obstacle to cross and he did just that.

Most people will always have obstacles in their path, while truly successful people see the objectives and their goals. They see what lies beyond the obstacles. They see the end game, and this allows them to endure any temporary setback.

Every failed business should be used as an opportunity to make wiser decisions. An optimistic business owner never takes a myopic approach to business and is never ambiguous in his business decision. His optimism is his ability to see the other side of the coin; to see opportunity in every disaster.

Thomas Edison once faced a major disappointment when a fire burnt most of his life's work, which exceeded $2 million--at the time, that was a great fortune.

The next day when Edison surveyed the fire damage he said, "There is great value in disaster. All of my mistakes are burned up; thank God we can start anew." Edison lived an optimistic life and because of it he experienced great success in his business and in his personal life. Edison developed a high tolerance for failure and as a result, changed the world.

These eight points are crucial in the life of an entrepreneur. There are many examples of successful entrepreneurs who have developed many of these characteristics and became successful. If you desire to be successful in business you must have a good understanding of your leadership ability.

The art of good leadership is the ability to draw on specific characteristics when needed. As an entrepreneur you will face many situations that will pose challenges for you. Therefore, your imagination and determination coupled with your resolve to act is the first step in meeting your challenges face to face.

In addition, doing what others are afraid of doing by stepping out and taking risks, using your talent, as well as your inner desire to achieve, will pave the road on your way to success. These characteristics will give you the ability to look failure in the face and smile, to overcome every obstacle and to accomplish whatever you put your hands to.

Finally, being confident and optimistic will give you the ability to soar like the eagles and rise to higher heights. These eight characteristics are vehicles in which successful entrepreneurs move from employee to employer and from success to success.

Chapter 1

CHAPTER 2

Barriers Facing Entrepreneurs

Entrepreneurs face many barriers in their businesses. Some of the barriers which hinder entrepreneurial development are:

- Start-Up Cost
- Long Hours
- Fear of Failure
- Physical and Emotional Stress
- Personal Resistance
- Fear of the Unknown
- Fear of Risks
- Lack of Confidence to Tackle the Venture
- Competition
- Resistance to Change
- Fear About New Ideas
- Negative Influences

All entrepreneurs face some of these barriers at one time or another during their business life. All barriers are either internal or external. External barriers may be factors beyond your control such as government and bank regulations, the strength of your country's economy and its markets, and the variability of government support.

Internal barriers, on the other hand, are your personal fears that can be controlled and conquered. Internal barriers are the greatest paralyzers of you realizing your dreams. The most disabling of all internal barriers is the barrier of fear. Fear immobilizes individuals from moving out of the realm of unemployment and into the joys of entrepreneurship.

Internal barriers are the more difficult of the two barriers because you must come to grips with your fears and shortcomings. Once you have faced your fears, you would be one step away from realizing your dreams and becoming a successful entrepreneur.

High start-up cost is the number one barrier facing entrepreneurs. Most potential entrepreneurs never realize their dreams of becoming successful business owners because the barrier of having a high start-up cost has always been a major setback.

Often young entrepreneurs only see the glamour in being their own boss, but the sacrifices sometimes are too great. Long hours and countless nights away from family and friends take a toll and sometimes discourages potential entrepreneurs.

When it comes to starting something new, most people don't because they are afraid of failing. Even entrepreneurs who have great business ideas and a positive outlook on their future can be paralyzed by the fear of failing.

Other factors such as stress, fear of risks, and lack of confidence also play a role as a hindrance to successful entrepreneurship and small business development. Starting your own business will demand a change in your lifestyle. However, most people tend to resist change, which is an internal barrier that we all must face. As a potential entrepreneur you must also be on your guard against the negative influence barrier. This barrier is placed in front of us by people we are closest to, and it is often because they fear change, too. Change can be frightening and intimidating for everyone, but until you overcome any fear of change, you may not reach your full potential for success.

All barriers can be overcome if you are determined. It is up to you to face your fears head-on and be willing to do whatever it takes to win.

Steps in Developing a Business

There are twelve crucial steps listed below that an entrepreneur must take during establishing a business. First, always remember all organizations and organisms go through a cycle of **birth, maturity and death.**

This cycle, when applied to business, translates into **inception, growth, and decline.** The first eight steps are related to the inception of the business. They are the steps taken to make your business a reality. Steps nine, ten and eleven are related to the growth of the business. These are the steps that determine whether your business is successful or not. These three steps should be monitored closely because they deal with the day-to-day operation of the business. Finally, the twelfth step is related to keeping your business from dying.

1. Identifying the opportunity (what)
2. Identifying the need for a product/service
3. Researching & analyzing the opportunity (what purpose)
4. Researching the market
5. Identifying the business (How)
6. Deciding on a business venture
7. Planning the business (Business Plan)
8. Who, What, When & How
9. Developing the business
10. Raising funds, allocating tasks, taking action
11. Monitoring & evaluating progress
12. Checking on progress, adjusting plan as necessary.

Before you can begin to develop your business, you must first determine if there is a market for the product/services you would like to offer and determine how you will meet this need.

Research is vital for the success of any start-up business. Therefore, you must properly and thoroughly research your market and the industry to have a better understanding of your market trends. Now identify what business you will get into. Isolate the market segment you will reach and examine any service. How will you reach your target market?

Begin to accumulate data from your research for your business plan. As discussed earlier, your business plan is needed before you start your business. You need to know who will run the business, if you will need employees, what function they will serve and how soon you will need them.

Another important factor is how you secure financing for your business. We will discuss this topic further on in this chapter.

Your business plan should be used as a yardstick to monitor your business progress and should be adjusted as necessary. A quarterly review should be done to ensure that your business performance is on track with your plan.

Factors Affecting the Entrepreneur

Globalization & Entrepreneurship

Being a global player in the new world economy requires entrepreneurs to have a better understanding and appreciation of the evolution of world economies over the past century. During this century, First-World economies have evolved from being labor intensive to being capital-intensive and now knowledge-intensive. A knowledge-based economy is primarily driven by entrepreneurship since individuals are the ultimate source of organizational and national knowledge.

As an entrepreneur, to position yourself to benefit from globalization you must be aggressive and committed to reinventing yourself and the way you do business. Part of this self-restructuring is understanding the importance of knowledge and how it affects business decisions. Decide whether you will be an employee or an employer. Being an employer means moving into the realm of entrepreneurship. Becoming an entrepreneur means planning your business objectives and strategies, short and long term. This book is designed to do just that: help you plan your business.

For entrepreneurs to survive and remain competitive in the globalized arena, they must not remain static. A strong and vibrant entrepreneurial culture that thrives on creativity is the cornerstone for a healthy economy. In a progressive economy, new ideas generate new economic growth. Without the constant infusion of ideas, economies will be become stagnant, anemic and lose its competitive edge.

In fact, innovations must be the driving force to expand the economic pie, increase productivity, and generate new wealth in the new global economy.

The new economy must also embrace a new kind of management. Knowledge management is what is needed to give an organization a competitive advantage over its competitors. Knowledge management is defined as the processes necessary to generate, capture, codify, and transfer knowledge across the organization to achieve a competitive advantage. This topic will be discussed further in the book under the heading management.

Entrepreneurship in the new millennium requires individuals to be greater risk-takers and innovators with a global perspective to business. Entrepreneurs who desire to be successful must not take on a myopic view of doing business but consider the possibilities of international business that cross trade barriers and cultures.

In fact, it was Adam Smith who argued some 200 years ago, in his book *Wealth of Nations,* that a society which encourages entrepreneurship would result in a more stable, free, and prosperous economy than one planned by the state.

In the new economy, businesses that are globally competitive will have a better chance of surviving, and those that are not will have to reinvent themselves to stay in business or die. This may be a hard pill to swallow, but it is reality. For businesses to survive in the global market, they cannot and must not be run the way they were a hundred years ago.

As an entrepreneur, globalization's invisible hand will add greatly to your success if you have a better understanding of ideas and how they impact society at large, education and its profound effect on the workforce, technological change which enhances efficiency and effectiveness, finance which is the ability to manage money and national policies which encourages or hinder free trade.

Globalization allows products to be made and sold anywhere around the world. It also forces companies and entrepreneurs to re-evaluate their entire supply chain because it gives them the opportunity to have products and services produced in developing countries at a much lower cost than in developed countries.

With the modernization of information technology and the emergence of global commerce, entrepreneurs who understand the power of effective utilization of both will have a competitive advantage over their rivals. Businesses which embrace technology as a main pillar in their business strategy will, no doubt, operate more efficiently and effectively than businesses that don't.

In fact, with a computer, an Internet connection, and a little know-how, individuals and companies in the most remote locations on earth can compete and collaborate globally. This process has changed the world as we know it and has made access to information timelier and easier and gave many individuals an opportunity to become successful entrepreneurs.

The flow of information, data and knowledge through new mediums of telecommunication has resulted in economies emerging to an interconnected global economy, making global e-commerce possible in the grasp of those who ordinarily would not have had the opportunity.

In the struggle for survival, the fittest win out at the expense of their rivals because they succeed in adapting themselves to their environment. As these global trends progress it is becoming obvious that only those organizations which understand, and plan accordingly, will survive and flourish in the new global economy.

Information Technology in Business

All new start-up businesses and existing businesses must factor in the use of technology within their businesses if they want to benefit from the use of information technology. Technology makes business efficient and relevant. Without the use of modern technology, businesses will not operate as smoothly and effectively as they should. In fact, it is virtually impossible to exist in today's business climate without the proper implementation and use of technology.

If you desire to be a successful entrepreneur, having an understanding and appreciation of information technology is critical. In the realm of technology, there are four key components of an IT strategy: hardware, software, networking and data. The IT strategy should be secondary to the organizational business strategy. Once the organization is clear about its business strategy (who, how, what), it can then determine what components of the IT strategy will be appropriate for it to fulfill its organizational goals.

In planning a successful business, you must develop an IT strategy that will complement your business strategy. Most people make the mistake of thinking that they can start a business without properly developing an IT strategy. It is important that you do not make this tragic mistake. Starting a business without a proper IT strategy will only cost you money for time wasted in the long run. Do not attempt to start and/or operate your business without a relevant IT strategy. If you don't know how to develop an IT strategy, seek out an IT professional who will be able to assist you in this regard.

When starting your business planning, it is important to clearly outline your business strategy so that you can properly develop your organizational and IT strategy. Your business strategy should define the overall goals and objectives of the company (*your business strategy is a part of your business plan*). An IT strategy can only be properly implemented if the organization clearly defines goals and objectives the company is trying to achieve. The overall goals of an IT strategy are to support and complement the business goals and objectives.

Once these goals and objectives are determined, the company can then outline or formulate its organizational and IT strategy (i.e. how many employees will be needed to accomplish the company's goals and objectives) What type of information system will be needed to reach the organizations goals? (i.e. network, computerization of every department, web portal, etc.)

If the business strategy is not clearly outlined, the organization will experience a high degree of organizational deficiency and chaos. There will be the consequence of over or under estimating the company's IT needs. The company may find itself spending more than is needed to meet its needs.

On the other hand, in the absence of a clearly defined business strategy, the company may think that a skeleton IT infrastructure will be enough when it needs a more complex IT network that integrates its entire value chain process and departments. It is important as an entrepreneur that you have a clear understanding of the relationship between the business strategy and the IT strategy. It is important for you to remember that an IT strategy can only be developed once the business strategy is properly outlined and defined.

For example, if a carmaker has a strategy of building a car that goes 250 mph and is clear about what he wants in the design, he can then build the components to facilitate his strategy.

If a new start-up business strategy is to sell products over the Internet, its IT strategy must be developed to complement its organizational plans. The business must develop a web portal that can facilitate e-commerce. Further, the business must ensure that it has the proper IT infrastructure in place to accommodate traffic to the site. In addition, the business must ensure that once a sale is made online, its departments are connected through a network to facilitate the transactions.

For example, once the sale is made online, the accounts department receives notice of the payment immediately. The warehouse or inventory department receives notice of the product purchased. The shipping department is also notified of the sale which receives the item from the inventory department, and they prepare the item to be shipped. Once the product is shipped, a notice is sent from the inventory department to suppliers about the quantity of products left on hand. The supplier then ships out new inventory when the inventory reaches a certain level and the cycle repeats itself.

This scenario gives you an idea of how to plan and properly implement your IT strategy. As a small business, your IT strategy may not be as complex as the one stated earlier in the beginning. Nonetheless, if you intend to grow your business, your long-term IT strategy must take in consideration the complex scenario, as outlined earlier.

It is not my intention to go to in depth about how to formulate a complex IT strategy. Such a topic is out of the scope of this book. However, if you want to be successful in your business, my advice is to get as much information as possible about the proper implementation and use of an IT strategy and how it can positively affect the overall performance of your business.

Information systems bring a great degree of organization and structure to businesses and automate business operations. Computer networks allow your staff to work together on specific and various projects simultaneously. Networking is the path by which an organization channels information to its various departments and even supplies.

As stated earlier, software is one of the four key components of an IT strategy. For your computer hardware to function, it must be powered by software. Once you've decided on your business strategy, you can now decide on which route you will take regarding the use of software in your business.

On the one hand, many organizations customize their own software to meet their needs. On the other hand, some businesses can function fine with an off-the-shelf software package. There are many off-the-shelf software packages that can help you organize and run your business. Software such as Quick Books© and Peachtree© are available and can be effective in automating your business.

As an entrepreneur, you should have at least the basic knowledge of how to operate a computer system. If you are computer illiterate, my advice to you is to find a school that will provide you with basic training in computers literacy.

In the start-up section of your business plan, a provision is made for the purchase of computer systems and software. The cost of basic training can be included in the overall computer cost.

Internet & E-Commerce

Before we talk about the Internet, it is important that we define what the Internet is. The Internet is a global, interconnected network of computers cooperating with each other to exchange data using a common software standard known as hypertext markup language or HTML. Through telephone wires, fiber optic cables and satellite links, internet users can share information in a variety of forms. The internet is as important to a business today as money is to a bank. The information super-highway has revolutionized the way businesses are operated and managed.

The Internet is the backbone for electronic commerce, or e-commerce, in which transactions occur instantaneously over a network and involves virtually no paper. E-business is the term more typically used to describe business conducted over the

Internet. E-business can be categorized into several main categories, B2B or business-to-business, where e-commerce is conducted between businesses, B2C or business to customer, where e-commerce is conducted between businesses and their customers, and finally, C2C, or customer to customer, where business or electronic transactions are conducted between customers. If you are a bit confused over the model C2C, this e-business model is what is used by eBay, where customers can go online and buy products from other customers.

The evolution of the Internet over the years has moved from an information based medium to an electronic commercial-based medium, where companies develop a unique ability to interact with its customers through graphics and text coupled with features that allowed electronic commerce or online sales.

Because of the Internet and its far-reaching possibilities, businesses across the globe were forced to rethink their business model.

Businesses, which were traditionally brick-and-mortar, or which had a physical presence, had to reinvent themselves and craft a new bricks and clicks business model, which combined an e-business with a physical business.

This new business model gave entrepreneurs a new avenue for generating new sales, reaching customers ordinarily out of reach; giving customers access to more information to make better decisions about their products and or services

The Internet made information about products or services more accessible to the global market. It also serves as the dividing line whether some businesses fail or succeed. Businesses that are revolutionary in their operations embrace the use of the world wide web and have a greater chance of succeeding than those which don't.

In today's business environment, a web presence has become a critical part of business operations and serves as an important factor in an organization disseminating information about its products and services. If you want to be taken seriously in the business world, your business should have a web presence. A web presence makes your company accessible, makes e-commerce possible and places your business in the living room where everyone has a computer and Internet access.

The Internet essentially brings a company's products and services to you instead of you having to go to the company by virtually diminishing the relevance of geography.

E-commerce is the process of buying and selling goods and services over the internet. E-commerce has changed the face of business globally forever.

New market opportunities have opened, and business operation expenses have now been reduced because of a lowering of overhead expenses due to the Internet. E-commerce has also made it easier for new entrepreneurs to enter into different markets with little startup costs. The Internet also allows your products and services to be available 24 hours a day, seven days a week, giving your customers constant access to your business as well as your products and services.

E-commerce is also a major component of a globalized economy that accounts for more than $2 trillion. It is estimated that this trend will grow to $4.3 trillion by the year 2020. A wise entrepreneur can identify opportunities and seize them.

With global opportunities opening because of the Internet, existing businesses must begin to re-position themselves to take advantages of the new opportunities in their domestic as well as foreign markets.

The Internet is the most effective way of tapping into new markets or creating new opportunities for your business. New, start-up businesses must take advantage of the Internet from inception. The Internet must be an integral part of the of your business strategy because the success of your business is directly related to it.

Legal Structure

Many entrepreneurs struggle with the decision of whether to remain sole proprietorship, partnership or form a corporation. When it comes to forming a corporation, the advantages outweigh the disadvantages. Some of the advantages of incorporating are:

1). A corporation has the most enduring legal business structure. If a sole proprietor or partner dies the business ends or it may become involved in various legal entanglements. Since a corporation has a life of its own, it may continue on regardless of what may happen to its individual officers, managers or shareholders. Ownership of the business may be transferred, without disrupting operations, through the sale of stock.

2). Sole proprietorship and partnerships are subject to unlimited personal liability when it comes to business debt. Creditors of the business can hold the owners of the business personally liable for debt and can move to seize the proprietor's or partner's home, savings or other personal assets. The shareholder of a corporation has only the money he has put into the company to lose, and usually no more.

3). Capital can be more easily raised with a corporation. This may be accomplished through the sale of stock or other equity interests. With sole proprietorships and partnerships, investors are much harder to attract because of the personal liability issue. For example, if the investor in a sole proprietorship (or some forms of partnerships) wants a share of the business for his capital contribution, he could become subject to a demand on his personal assets from creditors if the business becomes insolvent.

4). In a partnership each individual general partner may bind the business to arrangements that may result in serious financial difficulty. A corporation's shareholders cannot legally commit the company by their acts simply because they have invested in it.

5). This is the most common and most important corporate structure. The corporation is a separate legal entity that is owned by stockholders. A general corporation may have an unlimited number of stockholders that, due to the separate legal nature of the corporation, are protected from the creditors of the business. A stockholder's personal liability is usually limited to the amount of investment in the corporation and no more

The most important advantage of incorporation is that it gives its stock-holders limited liability. Since the corporation is a separate legal entity, its stockholders are protected from the debts and liabilities of the corporation.

The advantages of a corporation are:

1. A corporation has unlimited life. If an owner dies or sells his interest the corporation will continue to exist and do business.

2. Ability to easily establish insurance and retirement plans.

3. Ownership of corporation is easily sold or transferred through sale or transfer of stock.

4. Capital can be raised through sale of stock.

5. A corporation has centralized management which may remain in place after sale of the business.

Funding

One of the primary reasons for writing a business plan is to raise funding for your business venture. No business can exist without money. Money is the life blood of your business. Without it you only have an idea written down on pieces of paper. It is important that you approach funding of your business venture with the ultimate seriousness.

The first thing you must determine when approaching funding for your business is how much money you will need to get your business started. One of the primary reasons for many small businesses' failures is undercapitalization. Many entrepreneurs underestimate the amount of cash flow needed for their business to survive.

One common mistake made by entrepreneurs in a startup business is that they usually forget to factor in contingencies needed if their business does not make any money in the first three to five months of operations. **DON'T MAKE THIS MISTAKE**. Remember, nothing in business is guaranteed. Starting and maintaining a business is a risk, but make sure your risk is calculated.

You must plan for the bad times just as you would for the good times. Therefore, when determining the amount of startup capital, you need, make sure you factor in enough cash to pay salaries, rent, and cover your operating expenses for a considerable period, preferably three to six months.

Most lending institutions understand the importance of and the need for contingencies and probably will consider it a merit for planning wisely. Safety nets are always a plus in the eyes of lending institutions.

What Lending Institutions Look For

Many people think that lending institutions are impressed with rosy business plans. A business plan means nothing to a lending institution if you, the entrepreneur, do not know what is in it. It is important that you do not fall victim to this scenario. If you are going to take the route of having someone else write your plan, you should be a part of building the plan every step of the way.

When lending institutions interview you regarding funding, they need to feel comfortable with the fact that you have an in-depth understanding of your business venture. They need to know that you understand your industry trends, know your market, market segmentation, channel of distribution, sale strategy and funding strategy. Always remember, lending institutions do not have money to waste. So, it is on you to prove to them that you deserve the funding you are asking for.

Types of Funding

Essentially, there are two types of funding: **Equity Funding** and **Non-Equity Funding.** Equity funding is money acquired from investors for capital investment which requires that you to give up partial ownership of your business. Equity funding usually comes from partners or shareholders (if your business is a corporation and you are selling shares). Non-equity funding is funding that provides capital investment for your business without requiring that you relinquish a piece of your business. Non-equity funding usually comes from banks, venture capitalists or even family and friends.

Non-equity funding is a loan given to your business with hopes of receiving the initial capital invested plus interest over a period of time.

The advantages of non-equity funding are that you retain full ownership of your business and full control over the direction and management of your company. This compares to equity funding, where your shareholder/partner has a say in the way the company is being managed. Equity partners are part owners of the business and more than likely will want to give an input in the direction of the business.

One of the big advantages of equity funding is that there are no loan payments to make. If the business does not turn a profit or even goes bankrupt, the risk is all on the investor. However, with non-equity funding, banks and other lending institutions request collateral to protect their investment. It does not matter if your company turns a profit or not, their interest is usually secured.

If you have the means, another option of funding is available to you. Self-financing is where you, the entrepreneur, provide your company with the total funding for your business venture. Self-financing gives you the ultimate control of your business without having to worry about repaying a business loan or without giving up part of your business to shareholders.

This method of funding, even though it gives you a great deal of freedom, can put your personal cash flow in jeopardy if your business fails. This method, according to experts, isn't always the best method of financing. It is never a good idea to deplete your personal funds for a startup business.

Top 10 Reasons for Failing in Business

There are many reasons why small businesses fail within the first three years. There have been many studies where researchers have tried to find the reasons behind theses failure. In fact, statistics show that 90% of small business failures are due to a lack of knowledge or skills on the part of the entrepreneur. No one who starts a business believes that their business will fail. In fact, they believe the exact opposite. Most entrepreneurs, if not all, dream of making millions of dollars. However, these dreams are usually put to the test when the reality of the business starts.

After reviewing many expert opinions and their suggested reasons behind most business' failures, below is a list of our top ten reasons behind the failure of small businesses.

1. Capital Underestimation

The primary mistake for many failed businesses is capital underestimation or having insufficient operating funds. Entrepreneurs who do not calculate their start-up and operating needs will find themselves in financial crisis and be forced to close their business before they even have a fair chance to succeed.

2. Overexpansion

Entrepreneurs who feel the need to expand rapidly usually find that in the end, their business is short lived. Many business owners also get excited when their businesses experience above normal sales over a particular period. Do not be too hasty to expand. A slow and steady growth is optimum for your business future.

3. Failure to Control Cost.

Many startup businesses fail because of failure to control excessive spending. It is important that you track the money coming into and out of your business. Make sure that less money is going out than is coming in.

4. Poor Management

Another major cause for business failure, is poor managerial skills. Entrepreneurs who seek to start new business ventures but lack the necessary expertise in important areas such as management, finance, and marketing, will face the demise of their business. If you lack managerial skills it is important that you seek the necessary training or seek to hire someone who can fill the gap.

5. Poor Marketing

Many entrepreneurs underestimate the power of marketing. You can have the best product or service in the world, but if no one knows about your product or service, it will never sell. Marketing keeps your products selling and money flowing into your business. It's crucial that you do it well.

6. Poor Location

Location, location, location is essential to the survival of your business. If no one knows how to find your business, then you are doomed. Failure to identify a good location will cost you your business in the end. The location of your business should always be accessible to your customers and potential customers. If your location is poor, so will be your sales.

7. Failure to Change and Adapt.

Adaptability is a characteristic of a good entrepreneur. In today's business climate it is important that you understand that change is the only constant in life. Entrepreneurs who fail to change and adapt will end up with a relic for a business. Smart business owners recognize opportunities and are flexible enough to adapt to changing times which is the key to surviving in today's business climate.

8. No Web Presence

Start-up businesses which fails to see the need for a solid web presence do not understand today's business climate. Every business should have a professional-looking and well-designed website. A website enables users all over the world to easily find out about your business and how to access your products and services.

9. Failure to Meet Customers' Needs

The customer is the central focus of all your business activities, therefore, the customer should be appreciated at all cost. You must do whatever it takes to keep them loyal. If you don't treat your customer special, someone else will.

10. Incompetent and Unproductive Employees.

Your employees are on the front line of your business. Therefore, it is essential that you hire employees who are properly trained and able to complete the tasks expected of them. If your employees need additional training in customer relations, don't hesitate to get them the training they need. Remember, your business is only as good as your employees.

The list above gives you the top ten reasons why business fail. It is important that you study these reasons and try to avoid falling victim to them. The success of your business depends on your ability to make wise decisions and avoidance of these obvious pitfalls.

Review Worksheet

This worksheet will assist you in the development of your new business venture. Please answer all questions as best as possible.

1. Who or what is an entrepreneur?

_____

_____

2. What are the characteristics of an entrepreneur?

_____

_____

_____

3. What are some of the factors that hinder entrepreneurship?

_____

_____

_____

4. What barriers do entrepreneurs face?

_____

_____

_____

5. What are six of the twelve steps in developing a business?

1) _____

2) _____

3) _____

4) _____

5) _____

6) _____

6. What are the factors that affect the entrepreneur or enterprise?

_____

_____

_____

7. Why is it important to have technology in business?

_____

_____

_____

8. What are the four key components of an IT strategy?

_____

_____

_____

9. What are the benefits of the Internet to your business?

_____

_____

_____

10. What is E-Commerce?

_____

_____

11. What is the size of the E-commerce industry?

_____

_____

_____

12. What are the categories of E-Commerce?

_____

_____

_____

13. What are the types of legal structure?

_____

_____

14. What are the advantages of a Partnership?

_____

_____

_____

15. What are the benefits of a Sole Proprietorship?

_____

_____

16. What are the benefits of a Corporation?

_____

_____

17. What are the two types of funding?

_____

_____

18. What do lending institutions look for?

_____

_____

_____

19. What are the top ten reasons for failing in business?

_____

_____

_____

20. What are the advantages of equity funding?

_____

_____

_____

Self-assessment for Getting into Business

The following questionnaire will encourage creativity and identify your likes and dislikes.

    1. What are you good at?

_____

_____

_____

_____

    2. What do you struggle to do, or find difficult?

_____

_____

_____

_____

    3. What do you always avoid having to do?

_____

_____

_____

4. What type of work do you really enjoy doing?

_____

_____

_____

_____

5. What type of business do you find interesting?

_____

_____

_____

6. Why do you want to start your own business?

_____

_____

_____

_____

7. What are your strategic goals for your business?

_____

_____

_____

_____

8. How do you plan to accomplish your goals?

_____

_____

_____

_____

9. Where do you see yourself in 5 years?

_____

_____

_____

10. What do you want for yourself, financially and personally?

_____

_____

_____

_____

11. Are you willing to put in long hours in a new business?

_____

_____

_____

_____

12. What experiences do you bring to a new business (managements etc.)?

_____

_____

_____

_____

Chapter 2

CHAPTER 3

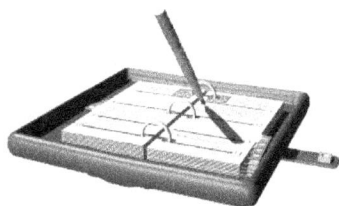

"The will to win is important,
but the will to prepare is vital."

– Joe Paterno

Guidelines for Developing A Marketing Plan

What is a Market?

A market is the total number of individuals and organizations that will be interested in buying or using the goods and services your organization provides.

It is also important to recognize that the term 'market' does not only refer to a single type of possible customer. A number of different markets are identifiable.

1. The Consumer Market
2. The Institutional Market
3. The Industrial Market
4. The Government Market
5. The International Market

What is a Market Segment?

A market can be divided up into smaller "segments." The market of college students is divided into segments such as young men and women; age group (17-40); employed, unemployed, with car, without car, etc.

Each segment has its own features which may make it a likely or unlikely source for your product or services. Market segmentation allows your business to better satisfy the needs of your potential customers.

Market Research

Before you decide on a business venture, it is wise to find out more about your market and the type of image you want to project.

You should identify the market segment that has a demand for your products or services.

TO DO THIS, YOU NEED TO:

1. Identify a market for your products/services
2. Identify the members of your market.
3. Contact a reasonable number of them (survey, telephone, and questionnaire)
4. Find out what their views are on the kind of products/services you have in mind.
5. Identify your competition's strengths and weaknesses.
6. Draw a conclusion from your research and decide on the aim of your business.
7. Determine if your products/services are filling a need that is important to people?
8. Determine how much people are willing to pay to have this need fulfilled.
9. Determine what image you want to portray.
10. Determine what your logo, slogan and colors will be.
11. Determine how quality control will be achieved in all aspects of your business from making the product to how the phone is answered.
12. Determine where your business will be located.
13. Determine when you will begin operating your business.

The Four P's in Marketing

The four P's in Marketing that all businesses are centered around are:

PRODUCT is the good or service that a company is providing. How does your product or service meet a certain demand, or add value to the market?

PLACE which is the location of the business.

PROMOTION is the marketing aspect of the business. It is the form of advertising that a business employs and the way a business promotes itself.

PRICE is the value a business puts on a good or service.

At the center of the four P's, lies the **customer**. The customer is the determining factor for the P's. Before you can think about a product or service you must think about your target market.

A business must be strategically located where customers have easy access. Location must be considered with the customer in mind. Advertising and promotion must be also strategic. Target market and market segment must be channeled to get the maximum response. All promotion must be done with the customer in mind.

The price of a good or service must be done with the consideration of the type of customer you want to reach. The customer demand determines the price of a product.

The SWOT Analysis

SWOT is an acronym for: **Strengths, Weaknesses, Opportunities and Threats.** This analysis is used to assist the business owners in an assessment of where they are, what they can do internally and externally. It also assists in determining what their limitations are and the factors beyond their control. This analysis is very helpful to entrepreneurs who want to start a business. The SWOT analysis is like a gauging stick for new business entrants. It gives somewhat of an accurate assessment of the position of your business.

NOTE:

Strengths and **Weaknesses** are related to matters that are **INTERNAL** to your business, while **Opportunities** and **Threats** relate to **EXTERNAL matters**.

A Plan of Action

A Plan of Action is structured to assist you in:

- Having knowledge of your customer.
- Learning your competitors' strengths and weaknesses.
- Defining your goals and objectives.
- Setting time frames to reach your goals
- Dissecting your tasks into small segments
- Knowing how much money you need to start and operate your business, and how long it will take before you can expect a profit.

It should also include HOW, WHEN, WHERE, WHY & WHAT.

Distribution Channel

Getting your products to market is vital to the survival of your business. How will you get your products to market? How will the end user (customer) get your products? Methods used by companies to get their products to market vary depending on the size and strength of their sales force.

Consider Dell Computer Inc., For many years, Dell sold their computer systems directly to the end user, through telephone orders or through their website. Dell's direct distribution worked well for their business. However, other companies such as, Sony, Samsung and Hewlett Packard, use distributors or retailers like Best Buy and CompUSA. What works well for one company may not work well for another.

Amazon is now introducing drone delivery for its customers. This new channel of distribution has and will continue to revolutionize product delivery for customers around the world.

To determine what distribution channel is suitable for your business, you must understand your target market. The following questions will help you make the right decision when determining what distribution, you will use.

1. What distribution channel is already in place?
2. Are these distribution channels satisfying the target market?
3. If not, what alternatives can be used to replace the existing distribution channel?

As an entrepreneur, it is important that you understand the different types of distribution channels and which one will work best for your business.

- Wholesalers
- Retailers
- Direct (on-site)
- Direct Mail
- Telemarketing
- Internet (e-commerce) (Amazon/eBay)

- Agents
- Drone Deliveries

You are not limited to just one channel of distribution to get your product to market. When determining which method of distribution, you will use, always be mindful of profit and effectiveness. It does not make good business sense to use more than one channel to distribute your products if the cost associated with distribution will cut heavily into your profit margin and or effectiveness.

Industry Trends

Your business strategy should be crafted around your industry trends. It is important that you understand the tempo of your industry and its fluctuations based on the seasons. If you are starting a business and the industry trends shows that that industry is seasonal, then your business strategy should be an **in and out** strategy because such industries are high risks. The life cycle of the business is relatively short compared to other industry.

Don't ever start a business because you think the product or service will sell. Always do your homework. Look before you leap. Study and analyze the trends of businesses within that industry before you make your decision.

Product Life Cycle

As mentioned earlier, all businesses go through different stages in its evolution. This theory is also true for business products. (It is important to note that when we talk about products in this section, we are describing both products and services.) As products evolve and pass thorough the different stages, prices and profits are affected.

Traditionally, there are four stages in the cycle of a products life (illustrated in the diagram below): Introduction, Growth, Maturity and Decline. Some models add a fifth stage call saturation before decline. However, we will just use the traditional four for our discussion.

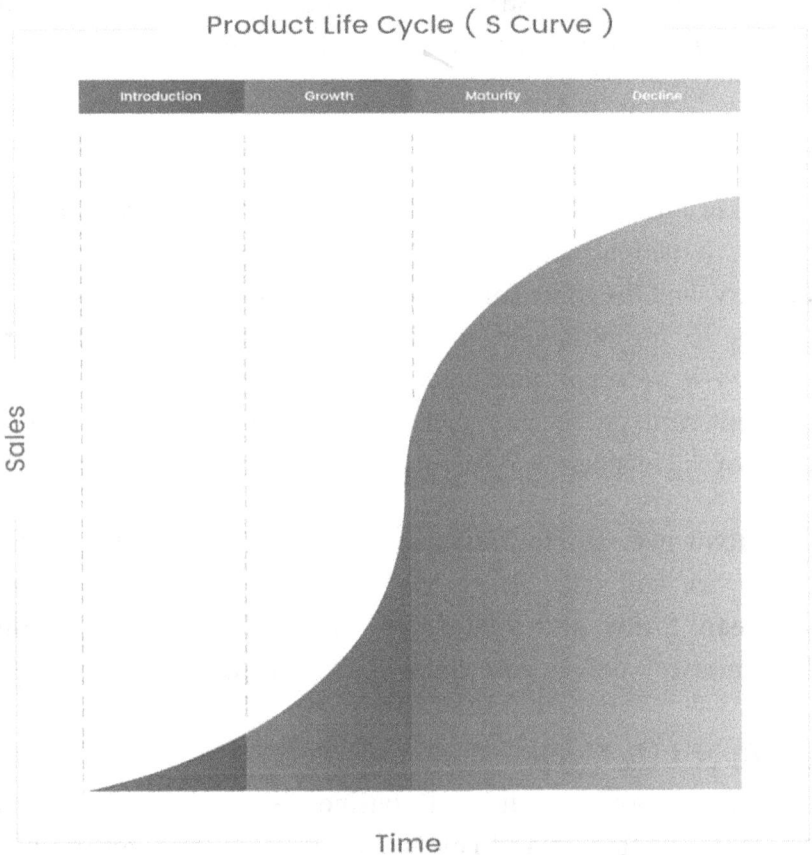

Product Life Cycle (S Curve)

| Introduction | Growth | Maturity | Decline |

Sales

Time

Table 3.0 Product Life Cycle (S Curve)

Introduction

For your business to be successful, it is critical that you understand the importance of the introductory stages of your product life cycle. During the introductory stage, your business will experience negative profits and a low sale volume. This is primarily because your product is new to the market and/or your business is new to customers. Getting your product established in the market will take time and a lot of effort by your marketing department.

More than likely your business will incur high marketing cost to position your product on the market stage. Most of your cost at this stage will be associated with promotions which include (radio, tv and newspaper ads, launch parties and internet ads.) During this stage, it is unlikely that your business will turn a profit. It is wise for you to plan carefully for this stage. Make sure you budget for the extra promotions and have contingency plan for operational expense during this slow growth stage.

Growth

This stage is the stage that most entrepreneurs love. This is the stage when their company is making money, and everything is going well. During the growth stage, businesses climb out of the red due to the increase in sales and profits. The growth stage is marked by a solid brand recognition and growing market share. Consumers love the product and clearly feel that it will bring them satisfaction in some way.

Rapid growth is realized at this stage and therefore it is important to plan wisely at this stage. Don't get carried away with excessive spending and try to expand the business at this time. Sit back and enjoy your growth.

Maturity

The maturity stage is the stage that most entrepreneurs don't plan for. During the maturity stage sales and profits peak because there are few first-time buyers for the product or services.

During this stage, the business is still experiencing increased sales but at a slower pace. At this stage, competition is strong and market share decreases because of new entrants to the market. It is important that you differentiate your products from that of your competitors.

During the maturity stage, the primary goal is to maintain market shares and extend the product life cycle. Entrepreneurs must understand that if they don't fight for their market share at this stage, they will lose ground in the market.

In differentiating your products from your competitors, your marketing mix should include:

Product - Product enhancements may be necessary with special features that set your product apart from the competitions.

Price - Price reduction is suggested because of rising competition.

Distribution - change your distribution channels and give incentives to resellers.

Promotion - promotion should be focused on strengthening your existing customer base and a winning new and old customer through special deals.

Decline

During this stage, sales begin to decline due to market saturation. Products become obsolete or lose their attractiveness in the market. This stage is marked by declining sales and declining profits. In the decline stage, the overall market begins to shrink, reducing the amount of profit to be shared in the market.

One example of a product that went into the decline stage is the type-writer. With the advent of the Personal Computer (PC), the typewriter became obsolete. Entrepreneurs must be crafty enough to understand when their products are in the decline stage.

It is important not to sit and mope about your declining sales and profits. If you don't act fast, your business will be obsolete like your product. There are some critical steps you can take when your business enters this stage.

1. Diversify your products or services quickly.
2. Sell you products in a different market (different state or country).
3. Lower pricing in order to liquidate stock.
4. Get out of the market.

Don't sit and wait for some miracle to happen, if your product is obsolete get out of the market quickly and look for new products that are in the growth stage and have a longer product life.

Marketing

Most small-business owners seem to underestimate the power of a proper marketing plan. In fact, marketing seems to be an afterthought in the minds of small business owners. Yet marketing is critical for the success of your business. According to the American Marketing Association, marketing is defined as" an organizational function and a set of processes for creating, communicating and delivering value to customers and for managing customer relationships in ways that benefit the organization and its stakeholders".

In other words, marketing is not just selling your products or services, but adding value to the consumer through your product or service while creating loyalty through customer relationship building. The traditional marketing concept focused on satisfying customers at a profit. As a small business owner, you might say, what's wrong with that? Let's examine this for a moment. This approach focuses on the short-term (profit) and does not seek to establish a longtime relationship with the customer and create value over time. We will elaborate on relationship marketing further in this section.

Many small business owners seem to make the mistake, when developing their business plan, only to market their business in the startup phase, which is a major factor for the failure of most small businesses. Marketing is an ongoing process, it never stops. As a successful small business owner, you must plan to market or sell your business at every opportunity.

Don't make the mistake of thinking everyone in a market or market segment knows about your business, and your products or services.

Even McDonald's who has sold more burgers than one can count, still spends millions of dollars on marketing and advertisement. The more people are reminded about your products or services through advertisement, the more the demand is for that product or service.

Marketing is the most powerful tool you can have as a small business owner. However, marketing can be very expensive for small startup companies. Therefore, it is critical that you plan properly for marketing your business.

If you are accessing funding from a bank, venture capitalist or financing the business yourself, it is important that your budget allows for three to six months of funds to market your business. It is detrimental to start a business and not have any monies allocated for the marketing of that business. Don't make this mistake. Poor marketing of your business is listed as one of the 10 reasons why businesses fail as stated earlier in this book.

After you have completed the planning stages regarding marketing and your business is up and running, there are some marketing principles that we will discuss in this section that are essential for your business to become a success.

In the next section we will discuss relationship marketing, market orientation and customer-centricity. We will briefly touch on each topic since a detailed discourse is out of the scope of this book. The following topics will be discussed further in my next book, *How to Operate a Successful Small Business.*

As an entrepreneur, gaining a competitive advantage in any market requires promoting your products and services continuously. Your promotions or ads must make consumers believe that your products or services will add value to their lives. You must brand your product or services as superior over your competition. Next, you must create a strong demand for your product or service through the repetition of marketing advertisement: television, radio, newspaper, Internet, etc.

In other words, you must use the Michael Porter theory of "differentiation" which attempts to create the impression that a company's products or services are different from that of others in the industry and, as a result, creating value over time for the customer. This differentiation can be a result of creating a brand image from technology, from a unique product feature, or from services that surpass expectation.

If you are to become a successful entrepreneur, don't try to follow the market, instead use your creativity in positioning your products and services in the market so that the market will follow you. In other words, don't just offer a service, offer superior customer service. Don't try to offer just a product but try to offer value to your customers. **Being different gives you a competitive advantage over your competitors.**

Being a copycat is easy; and for some entrepreneurs, this is the road most traveled. The problem with being a copycat is that your business gets lost in the crowd. Successful entrepreneurs understand that gaining a competitive advantage in a crowded market requires being singled out for either superior customer service, or high-quality, unique products, or both.

A strong competitive advantage can be gained through a strong bond with customers and consistently providing superior customer value to them.

Relationship Marketing

In marketing, the success of your business comes through customer retention, which is a result of strong customer relations. It is important as a small business owner not to seek profit at the expense of good customer relationships. Business owners who traditionally follow this method often find themselves losing their customer base.

There are several definitions that have been offered to explain relationship marketing. Relationship marketing is simply getting to know your customer so well that you can identify their needs and satisfy them. As a small-business owner, it is critical for you to know your customers and what their needs are and go above and beyond to satisfy those needs. This relationship is developed over time and is an ongoing process. Relationship marketing requires constant communication between the customer and the company.

Building customer relationships is vital for creating value over time for your organization. In fact, the customer relationship model displays how a customer moves from a prospect to an advocate as seen in the diagram below.

Customer Relationship Model

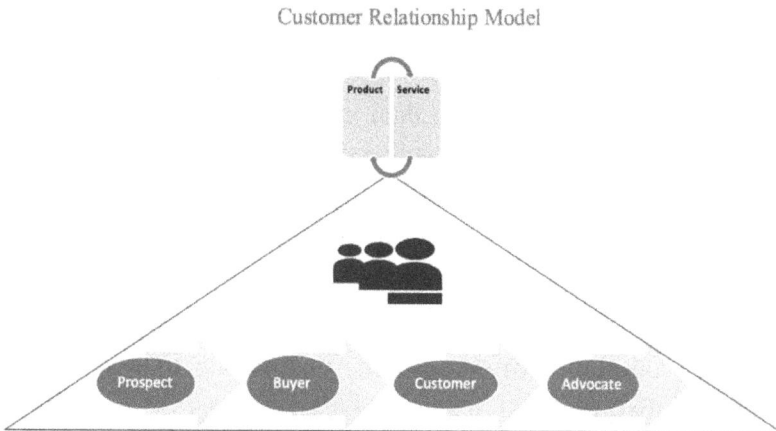

Running a small or medium size business gives you a competitive advantage when it comes to forming relationships with your customers. Since most small businesses have greater interaction with their customer base, opportunities are created to foster lasting relationships with the customers.

A top management guru, Peter Drucker, explains marketing with such clarity. He said, "The aim of marketing is to know and understand the customer so well that the product or service sells itself." Some management theorists are predicting that relationship between business and customers will become more important than products offered by those companies.

Even though in-depth discussion of this topic may be out of the scope of this book, it was important for you to have a brief review of a deeper level marketing.

Market Orientation

The new market-oriented process concept seeks to redefine the way businesses relate to their customers. Market oriented businesses seek to put customers first, create superior value for customers through quality products and services, and this eventually leads to increased overall business performance. Market oriented firms understand the importance of researching their niche market to provide the best possible products or services to their customers. Market orientation's central focus is satisfying or exceeding the customer's needs.

It also involves learning about your customers (what are their needs and wants?) and how you and your company may best satisfy those needs and wants. Market orientation also involves learning about your rivals and competitors. What type of services does your competitor offer? Are they satisfying their customers' needs? Are they going above and beyond to meet their customers' expectations? Are they satisfying their existing customer base?

To gain a sustainable competitive advantage in any market, successful entrepreneurs must understand the importance of market orientation and how it affects business success.

Customer-Centricity

Customer centricity seeks a new path in marketing and a new approach to dealing with the customer. Customer centric marketing seeks to satisfy the needs and wants of the *individual* customer rather than trying to meet the needs of a mass market. This new approach to marketing personalizes the methods in which a business interacts and satisfies its customers. Another name for this marketing approach is customer orientation.

A customer-oriented business in its service always puts customers first. In fact, a customer centric business knows and understands the quote made by Henry Ford when he said, "It is not the employer who pays the wages. Employees only handled the money. It's the customer who pays the wages." This quote encapsulates everything that was already said, and that will be said in this book. In other words, if you don't understand the importance of satisfying the customer, you are wasting your time in business. Without the customer, there is nothing.

As an entrepreneur it is important for you to always remember: the foundation and the lifeblood of your business is your customers. Since the customers is so critical to the success of your business, it is important for you to go beyond just trying to satisfy their needs; customer centricity demands that you become proactive and anticipate your customer wants and needs.

One of the ways to gain a competitive sustainable advantage in the new global economy is by the way you relate and interact with your customers. Don't ever make the mistake of becoming market myopic (forgetting customers' needs). One of the main reasons many businesses fail is because they failed to satisfy and anticipate their customer's needs. The key to having a successful business is to create customer loyalty or customer retention and turn those loyal customers in to advocates.

There are a few terms that I would like for you to become familiar with - during running a business. It is important for you to do some independent study of these terms so that they can become a part of your business culture and vocabulary.

- **Value(V)** what is value?
- **Customer Value (CV)** What is customer value?
- **Customer Oriented**. How to become more customer oriented.
- **Customer-Centric**. What is customer centric?
- **Market oriented**. How to become more market oriented.
- **Market Driven**. What is a market-driven company?
- **Business Process Orientation (BPO)**. Define business process orientation.
- **Quality**. What is quality?
- **Service Quality (SQ)**. What is service quality?
- **Service Quality Gaps**. What are service quality gaps?
- **E-Service Quality**. What is E-Service quality? **Value Proposition**. What is a value proposition?
- **Integrated Marketing Communication (IMC)** What is IMC?
- **Relationship Marketing**. What is relationship marketing?
- **Lifetime Value (LTV)**. What is lifetime value?

Even though we will not discuss the terms listed above in this book, I do believe that it is important for you as an entrepreneur to understand what these terms mean and how it relates to the success of your business. Starting and running a business is not an easy task. It requires work and much sacrifice. Don't ever make the mistake of thinking that success comes without a price.

If you want your business to be number one, you must work day and night at it. It is important for you research the definitions of these terms and how it relates to your business success.

Marketing Checklist

This checklist deals with the look of your business and how you express your corporate identity and positioning strategy.

    1. What will be the name of your business?

_____

    2. a.) Do you have a company logo?   Yes__No__

    3. b.) Do you have a business card?   Yes__No__

    4. c.) Do you have letterheads and envelopes?
    Yes__ No__

    5. Do you have brochures for your business?
    Yes__ No__

    6. Do you intend to have a web site?   Yes__No__

If yes, explain:

_____

_____

_____

    7. Are you an action-oriented person? Yes__No __

8. What will be your marketing approach?

Please note--You can choose more than one form of advertising.

a) Direct Advertising (radio, newspaper) ___

b) Mail Advertising ___

c) Telemarketing ___

d) Referrals ___

e) Trade shows & conferences ___

f) World Wide Web ___

g) Chambers of Commerce ___

h) Personal contacts ___

i) Yellow Pages ___

9. What is your Customer Advantage?
   (Better products or services, cheaper prices etc.)

_____

_____

_____

_____

10. Will your location be accessible to the public?
   Yes___No___

11. Where will your business be located?

_____

_____

12. What is your business structure?

Sole proprietor _____

Partnership _____

Limited partnership _____

Corporation _____

Non-profit _____

13. When is your starting date?

Month _____ Year _____

14. Does your business offer a product or a service?

_____

_____

_____

15. Describe briefly your products or services?

_____

_____

_____

16. What inventory will you need?

_____

_____

_____

_____

17. Do you intend to borrow monies from a bank? If so,

a) What bank? _____

b) What is the amount? _____

18. Who are your suppliers?

_____

_____

_____

19. Do they offer credit?   Yes __No __

20. Who or what is your target market?

_____

_____

_____

21. How will you educate the market about your products/services?

_____

_____

_____

22. What makes your products/services better than your competitors?

_____

_____

_____

23. What differentiate your products/services from your competitors?

_____

_____

_____

24. What stage in the product life cycle is your products/services?

_____

_____

_____

_____

25. What market will you position your product in?

_____

_____

_____

26. How can you apply the Relationship Marketing model to your products/services?

_____

_____

_____

27. How can you apply the Market Orientation model to your products/services?

_____

_____

_____

28. How can you apply the Customer Centricity model to your products/services?

_____

_____

_____

_____

Competitors

Name of Competitors?

_____

_____

_____

Market Share %?

_____

_____

_____

1. PRODUCTS OR SERVICES

a) How do the company's products or services differ from other products and services in the market place?

b) Do they offer a broad or narrow product line?

c) Do they emphasize quality?   YES ___ NO ___

2. PRICE

a) What is their average selling price? _____

b) What is their profit margin? _____

c) What type of discount do they offer? _____

d) Do they offer a low selling price? _____

3. PROMOTION

a) How well recognized are your competitors' brands?

_____

_____

b) How much do they spend on advertising?

_____

_____

c) Through which media do they advertise?

_____

_____

d) What other type of promotion do they use?

_____

_____

e) How many sales people do they have?

_____

_____

4. LOCATION

a) Where are they located? _____

b) Is location very important to the industry?

_____

5. MARKETING STRATEGY

a) Does the company cater to any particular segment of the market?

_____

_____

_____

_____

b) Does the company offer any unique products or services that make it different from other companies?

_____

_____

_____

_____

c) Do you offer a particular low price? YES___NO___

6. MARKET POSITION

a) What is your competitors' market share? _____

b) Have their sales been growing___, stable___, or declining___?

c) How successful are they?

7. MAJOR STRENGTHS AND WEAKNESS

a) What are the major strengths of your competitors?

_____

_____

_____

b) What are their major weaknesses?

_____

_____

8. Explain your market conditions. e.g. Technological advancements, change in demographics, competition?

_____

_____

_____

9. **What is the present stage of your industry: infancy, intermediate, or mature?**

_____

_____

_____

10. **What is your competition's channel/s of distribution?**

_____

_____

11. **How long have they been in business?**

_____

_____

12. **What are their competitive advantages?**

_____

_____

13. **What is your channel/s of distribution?**

_____

_____

CHAPTER 4

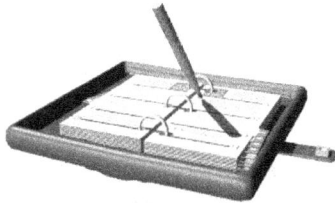

> "*A man who does not think and plan long ahead will find trouble right at his door.*"
>
> – Confucius (BC 551-BC 479)

Developing Your Business Plan

Answer the following questions.

1. Why do I need a business plan?

_____

2. What are the 4P's in marketing?

Write in the box below

The Marketing Mix
The Four P's of Marketing

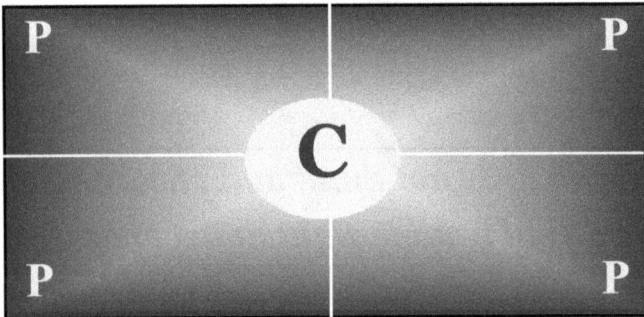

3. What does the <u>C</u> represent in the middle of the box?

_____

_____

_____

4. List the four P's of your business venture.

Write in the box below

P	P
P	P

Table 3.2 List the F P's of your Business Strengths, Weaknesses, Opportunities and Threat

5. What is the SWOT analysis of your venture?

Write in the box below

Strengths	Weaknesses
1._____	1._____
2._____	2._____
3._____	3._____
4._____	4._____
5._____	5._____
Opportunities	**Threats**
1._____	1._____
2._____	2._____
3._____	3._____
4._____	4._____
5._____	5._____

Table 3.3 SWOT Analysis Your Business

In the top left box, list five **STRENGTHS** of your business, operating division, sales territory or whatever you are analyzing. Be as honest as possible. Don't take any strength for granted; it might be something that your customers value and that your competition doesn't have or does. What differentiates you from your competitors? What do you do better, different, faster, cheaper, with higher quality or with a different spin? Be specific, not vague.

In the top right box list your **WEAKNESSES** - limitations, things you do not have, you cannot do, and don't do well. Be honest and realistic when listing your weaknesses.

The lower left box is for **OPPORTUNITIES**. What is the market NOT doing, what are your competitors NOT doing - what does the market need that your business could provide? Think in terms of what would benefit your customer - cheaper, easier, more convenient and faster...

The lower right box is for **THREATS** - the factors that can destroy your business. What products, prices, ads, or initiatives your competitors have that will put a strain on your business and make things hard for you?

Are they using the Internet to reach a broader customer base? Identify your threats and try to eliminate them.

6. Identify the SWOT analysis of Your Competition.

Write in the box below

Strengths	Weaknesses
1._____	1._____
2._____	2._____
3._____	3._____
4._____	4._____
5._____	5._____
Opportunities	Threats
1._____	1._____
2._____	2._____
3._____	3._____
4._____	4._____
5._____	5._____

Table 3.4 SWOT Analysis For Your Major Competition

A SWOT analysis identifies any strong points that can be duplicated and enhanced to make your organization more efficient and effective.

An accurate SWOT analysis also reveals any cracks in your competitors' wall of success. Once you can identify their weaknesses you can then proceed to avoid their mistakes and short-comings. If you have a good understanding of your competitors' weaknesses, you will always be one step ahead of them.

You also need to have a good understanding of the opportunities that are available to them, such as any special government contracts, special relationship with suppliers, etc.

Knowing your competitor's threats is crucial because you, too, may be faced with these same threats, such as change in governmental legislation or policies, diseases, changes in market trends, etc.

Developing A Marketing Plan

1. Who is your target market?

(Demographics and psychographs) please note:

DEMOGRAPHICS REFERS TO - income, gender, education, etc.

PSYCHOGRAPHICS REFERS TO - Values, philosophy, interests, characters that best describe your customer.

a) Demographics

_____

_____

_____

b) Psychographics

_____

_____

_____

c) You will be selling primarily to (check all that apply):

- Private sector _____
- Government _____
- Export Market _____

2. Who is your main competitor?

Name/s

_____

Address

_____

Price /Strategy

_____

Years in Business _____

Market Share _____

Product /Service Features

_____

3. What are the legal and governmental factors that will affect the market?

_____

_____

_____

4. What makes your product(s)/ services(s) different from your competitors?

_____

_____

_____

5. What are the benefits of your products/services to your customers?

_____

_____

_____

_____

6. What is your pricing strategy?

_____

_____

_____

What % mark-up? _____

Mark-up on cost _____

Suggested retail price _____

Competitive price _____

Premium price _____

7. **What is your customer's profile?**

_____

_____

_____

8. **Will your business be marketed on the internet?**

_____

_____

_____

9. **How does your product/s or service/s save your customers time and money?**

_____

_____

_____

10. **Will your product/s or service/s be marketed nationally, regionally or internationally?**

_____

_____

_____

11. How will you get your product/s or service/s to market?

_____

_____

_____

12. Are there any niche markets you can tap into?

_____

_____

_____

13. What is unique about your product's packaging?

_____

_____

_____

14. What form of advertisement will you use?

_____

_____

_____

15. How will your location affect you customers?

Management Team

Most entrepreneurs believe venture and lending institutions only look at numbers when it comes to funding new startup ventures. On the contrary, the management team is just as important to venture capitalists and lending institutions because the quality of your management team will determine how organized, effective and profitable your business becomes.

Lending institutions and venture capitalists know that financial projections in a new start-up business are only assumptions and are only a part of the entrepreneur's imagination. Therefore, more attention should be placed on your management team, the main force behind the organization.

The greatest asset in any organization is its people. Without people, no organization can be successful. Therefore, as an entrepreneur you must place tremendous effort in choosing and building a team of managers that meets your business needs.

The success and failure of your business will depend on the leadership ability of your management team. In choosing your management team, you must look for individuals who demonstrate the ability to be team players. No one person is more important than the other on a team. Your management team should be diverse with different skillsets and abilities; some in marketing, some in finance, some in sales, human resources and operations.

A diverse team of managers must also demonstrate that they understand and believe in the overall vision and objective of the organization. This is crucial for the success and growth of your business.

Management teams are important to businesses because they are responsible for the day-to-day operation. Your business plan will have more strength if your management team is highly experienced and qualified in their respective fields.

The strengths of your management team must be clearly articulated in your business plan. These strengths will strengthen your chances of raising capital for your business. Do not be afraid to mention the weaknesses of your management team, venture capitalist and lending institutions appreciate honesty and want you to be realistic in your plan.

The fact that you can identify weakness in your management team means that you can address and compensate for any short-fall your team may have. You should always look for ways to upgrade your management team skills. The more motivated and skillful your team is, the more efficient and profitable your business will become.

A good management team must have a great degree of versatility to adapt to constant market and unforeseen governmental changes. A dynamic management team will adjust quickly to any fluctuation in the market, advances in technology and changes in government legislations.

A static management team will be overcome because of failure to move with the changing tide. When choosing your team make sure they are dynamic, experienced and professional. If your business is to remain successful and viable, your management team will have to be the main ingredient.

When seeking to hire individuals to manage your company, always seek out the best. It is a smart entrepreneur who seeks to find individuals who are smarter than they are to run their company. Don't be intimidated if your managers are smarter than you. It is wise to surround yourself with people who are smarter than yourself.

Once you have selected your team, it is important that you trust them to do the job you hired them to do. If your management team feels they are not trusted, they will not perform at the level they should, and your profits will reflect that.

Giving your management team room to make decisions is not only healthy, but also vital for the success of your business. If your managers can't make decisions, then you don't need them. It may be best that your business remain a one man show.

Avoid power struggles with your managers; this will only lead to them becoming discouraged. Sometimes it may be best for you to take a back seat and allow them to drive, if that's what you hired them to do. You must allow your management team to develop synergy and this can only be developed by them working together, working out the kinks of the business without interference from you.

Stay away from hiring family and friends. Most often you are blinded by your relationship and overlook their skill level and competence. This is dangerous ground. Never hire someone because you like them or because you are related to them. Hire someone because they can meet the job specification and perform the task that they are hired to do.

Management Review

Let me reiterate: your management team is very important to the success of your business. Potential investors and lending institution pay close attention to the quality of your management. The quality of your team demonstrates your seriousness about your business and often determines whether your business receives start-up funding.

1. Who makes up your management team?

_____

_____

_____

2. Where were they educated?

_____

_____

_____

3. What are their past job experiences?

_____

_____

_____

_____

4. **List some of their accomplishments. Professional and personal?**

_____

_____

_____

_____

_____

5. **List the responsibilities of each manager.**

_____

_____

_____

6. **What is their reputation within the business community?**

_____

_____

_____

7. **What skills, abilities, and knowledge do they have?**

_____

_____

_____

8. Are they loyal to the business?

_____

_____

_____

_____

9. What motivates your team?

_____

_____

_____

_____

10. Are they team players? Can they work together?

_____

_____

_____

_____

11. Can your management team effectively manage crisis?

_____

_____

_____

12. What strengths does your management team possess?

_____

_____

_____

_____

13. What are the weaknesses of your management team?

_____

_____

_____

_____

14. What do you look for when hiring your managers?

_____

_____

_____

_____

Chapter 4

CHAPTER 5

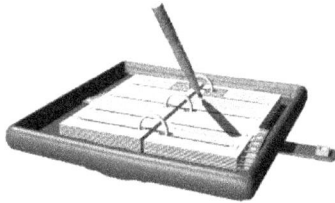

"Plan well before you take the journey.
Remember the carpenter's rule:
Measure twice, cut once."

– Unknown Source

BUSINESS PLAN OUTLINE

This Business Plan outline is designed to assist you in the development of your very own business plan.

Before we move into writing your business plan, a sample business plan out-line is provided below. Follow the instructions as closely as possible, then answer all questions provided in the actual business plan. After you would have answered all the questions, your data would need to be entered into a computer for finalization.

Business Plan Outline

COMPANY NAME
ADDRESS
CITY, STATE

Disclaimer

A business plan should include a disclaimer that limits distribution of the plan without the expressed consent of the company's owner.

Sample Disclaimer

This business plan is the property of ABC, Inc. Because it contains confidential information proprietary to ABC, Inc., no copies may be made of the contents herein. Neither can the contents be discussed by any party not previously authorized to discuss said contents by ABC, Inc., Officers. This copy must be returned to ABC, Inc. upon request.

Executive Summary

The executive summary is the foundation for the rest of the business plan. This section of the plan summarizes the entire document and should be prepared last because it contains information from the rest of the document. It is also important that your executive summary clearly states your objectives, or you will lose your reader. It should provide a clear picture of your plan for your readers. Do not make your executive summary too long.

Keep it short and to the point. It should be no longer than one page. Then the following paragraph should introduce your objectives and mission. It communicates the essence of what you offer. Try to emphasize the main points. Normally a chart is included that illustrates profit or return on investment.

Objective

Your objectives are your business goals. This section is where you set and clearly state the objectives of sales, profit, and market share. It is important that you set realistic objectives. Clearly state your goals, your level of sales and profits, your percentage of gross margin, growth rate and market share. Don't use unrealistic projections, be as concise as possible! It's how you will accomplish your mission.

Mission

A mission statement explains the reason for the existence of your business. Mission should not be confused with your objectives. Mission is the main thrust of the business. It is what your business is going to do such as: providing quality health services in the 21st century. It is the 'what you do' as oppose to the 'how you get it done'.

It is important to state your mission in a single paragraph or even a sentence. Keep it simple.

Company

This section explains your company products or services which are provided. It also explains the marketing channel and your target market. Do not overelaborate. Remain as brief as possible.

Company Ownership

This section describes the ownership of the company. Is it a partnership, sole proprietorship, or corporation?

Optional: A copy of your business license can be provided in this section.

Company History

When was the business founded? Who was the founder? Why was it founded? Has it progressed since being founded? Expand on the business product lines. Include sale, product and marketing information and how they have changed over time.

Products/Services

Give a detailed description of your product(s) you will be offering. If your business is service oriented, describe the type of service(s) you will be offering. It is important to be as detailed as possible because lending institutions need as much information as possible about your product(s) or service(s).

Location and Facilities

Describe the location of your business. Will your business be centrally located? Briefly describe the benefits of your location and whether the location is easily accessible.

Is public transportation available? Does your location have adequate street lighting? How much square footage will you use and what is the cost per square foot of your building? Do you have a lease arrangement and other information related to the facilities?

Promotion

Describe the type of promotional activities your business will be engaged in. How will you market your business? What medium will you use to promote your business? Will you have promotional giveaways or advertisements in certain magazines or publications? State as clearly as possible how you will you get your company's or product's name out there.

Pricing

What will be your pricing strategy? How did you arrive at pricing your products? Will the market be able to afford your products? What is the market average price for a similar product? Are you catering to a special niche or market? You must give justification for the price of your product.

Cost

What is the cost of purchasing your product? If you are manufacturing a product, list all the costs associated with producing your product. If your business is a service-oriented business itemize all the costs associated with providing your service.

Industry Analysis

This section gives a marketing background on the industry you are in. It provides information about the industry. For example, if you were in the Tourism Industry, this section would provide information on the tourism industry worldwide; Its growth rate and projections. This section requires extensive research that will provide your readers with a solid background of the industry's past, present and future.

Keys to Success

This section clearly outlines the reasons you decided to choose your business venture. What are some of your strong points that make the business special? These are your keys to success.

Technology

Explain how technology will affect your business. Will your business performance be positively or negatively affected using technology? How will technology be integrated into your business? Will the internet be a factor in selling your products or services.

Market Forecast

In this section you must include a spreadsheet of your market projections and charts to support it. This forecast is projected over a 5-year period.

Competition

Who will be your major competitor? What is the business strategy of your major competitor? How much of the market do they dominate? In what segments of the market do they operate? Will their market dominance affect your business? What threats and opportunities do they represent?

Market Share

Market share is determined by dividing company's sales by total market sales. Market share is useful in determining your position in the market and the position of your competition.

EXAMPLE OF MARKETSHARE:

Company Name	Annual Sales ($)
Company 1	10,000
Company 2	20,000
Company 3	40,000
Company 4	50,000
Company 5	40,000
Total	160,000

To determine Market share of Company 1, divide the total annual sales of $10,000 by the total market sale of $160,000; 10,000/160,000 = 0.0625.

Now multiply 0.0625 by 100 to determine percentage; 0.0625*100 = 6.25.

Market share of Company 1 = 6%.

Sales of Company 1 account for approximately 6% of total market sales.

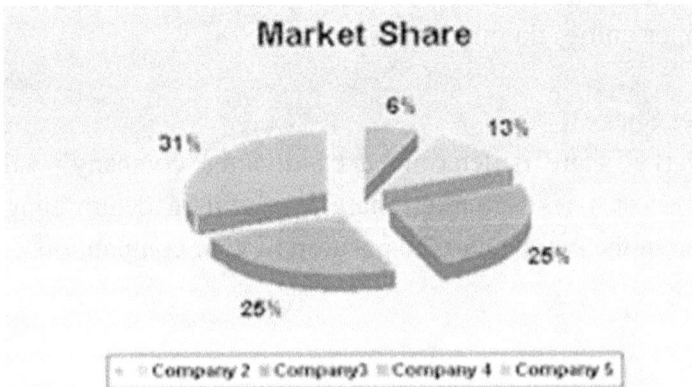

MARKET SHARE Company 1

Business Strategy

What is your business strategy as it relates to sales and marketing? What is your competitive edge?

What new technology gives you an advantage? Is your product superior to that of the competition? Is your marketing strategy better, price lower? Explain to the reader why he or she should invest in your business.

Market Strategy

Your marketing strategy should focus on a specific marketing segment, demographics - income level, gender etc. How will you distribute your product? Is your product distribution more efficient than that of your competitors? Are you distributing new products?

What are you doing that is better than your competition? State all your important marketing points. Through which media will you promote your business? Use the data from the "analyzing your competitors" form on page 43.

Market Segment

What market segment or subgroup of people or organizations sharing one or more characteristics will have a need for your product/s. Why will your business focus on a group of people? What makes that group of people of special interest to you?

Distribution Channel

How will you get your product to market? Will your product be sold through a retailer? Will your product be distributed through wholesale? Will your product be sold directly to the customer? When should the product or service be available? Describe the benefits of using a distribution channel.

SWOT Analysis

This section is used to evaluate the Strengths, weaknesses, opportunities, and threats in a business venture. SWOT involves specifying the *why* of your business venture and identifying the internal and external factors that are favorable and unfavorable to achieving that objective.

Sales Plan

This section not only explains what you sell but how you sell it. Are you a wholesaler, retailer or mail order business? Will your sales team work on commission or fixed salary? How are your sales people trained?

NOTE

This section also requires 5-year sales forecast for your business. See the example below.

Business Alliances

What strategic alliance do you have with any other company? Do you have a joint marketing or special arrangement with your wholesaler, distributors or any other company? How will these relationships improve your business?

Services

Not all businesses service their products. This category is only important to those companies that do. If your business is offering warranty on your products, then state how you will service these products under warranty.

Organization

This category gives an overview of how many employees are in the company; how many members are on the management team; and how many of those are founding members of the company.

Organizational Structure

This section displays the structure of your organization. The chart below gives an overview of the hierarchy of the business. List the important positions and the responsibilities of each one.

Management Team

Who are the most important members on your management team? Include a description of their background and experiences. What is their individual function with the company? Be as brief as possible. What are their strengths and their weakness?

Important note: A resume of all key personnel should be included in this section.

Name, Position Name, Position

Job Description

State the title and function of each member of your management team. What are their duties? What are the specifications and experiences required for each job title? President, Vice President, Human Resources Manager, Etc. Note: Please see example provided in appendix II

Management Team Gaps

Does your management team have weaknesses? Identify where the weakness is. State how you will fill the gaps. Weakness may mean lack of skill in a certain area or lack of qualification by any part of the team. Will the company provide the training for a member who needs it?

Other Considerations

State who is on your board of directors if any. Who is the major stock-holders if any and what are their roles in the business?

Financial Analysis

Show the financial highlights: Cash flow projections and net profit for the next 5 years. What is your return on investments and your internal rate of return? Use the same chart that is included in the Executive Summary. What type of accounting system will you use? Is it a single entry or dual entry system?

Financial Plan

Your financial plan will be highly scrutinized by your business plan reader. All the ideas, concepts and strategies discussed throughout your entire business plan forms the basis for, and should flow into, your financial statements and projections in some manner. Explain how you intend to finance your business. Bankers and investors are familiar with the correct content, organization and presentation of financial statements, and expect to see them in your business plan.

Start-up Capitalization

Do not use this section if your business is an ongoing business. If your business is new you should have a table showing start-up expenses, start-up assets, and start-up capitalization.

Start-up-Capitalization lists owner investment into the business; as well as bank loans and loans from other lending institutions. Start-up- Capitalization as shown in A NEW START also amortize your loan, display your interest rate and number of years for repayment.

Below is an example of your Start-up Capital as seen in your A NEW START software.

Start-Up Capital	
Start Up Cash	124,140
Owner's Investments	
Partner 1	50,000
Partner 2	0
Partner 3	0
Partner 4	0
Total Partner Contribution	50,000
Bank Loan	
Bank 1	150,000
Bank 2	0
Bank 3	0
Total Bank Loan	150,000
Other Loan	
Loan 1	0
Loan 2	0
Total Other Loan	0
Total Capitalization	200,000

What are Start-up-assets?

Start-up-assets are used to show a listing of all inventory as well as capital equipment such as furniture, machinery, vehicles, and office supplies. Start-up assets list all your building and real estate property. Building improvements are also a major part of your start-up-assets.

In your A NEW START software, each section of your assets has a contingency. A contingency is your buffer just in case your under-ester- mate your costs. Contingency is a percentage of the total of each section of start-up-asset.

Below is an example of your Start-up Assets as seen in your A NEW START software.

Fixed Assets Assumptions

Furniture & Equipment	Quantity	Price	Total
Desks	5	350	1,750
Chairs	10	60	600
Dividers	5	250	1,250
Other	5	150	750
Total Furniture & Equiptment Cost			**4,350**

Machinery	Quantity	Price	Total
Computers & Printers	5	950	4,750
Car	2	4,000	8,000
Item 3	0	0	0
Item 4	0	0	0
Total Machinery Cost			**12,750**

Real Estate	Quantity	Price	Total
Land	1	35,000	35,000
Construction	0	0	0
Building	0	0	0
Other Improvements	0	0	0
Total Real Estate Cost			**35,000**

Infrastructure Improvements	Quantity	Price	Total
Improvements 1	1	2,000	2,000
Improvements 2	0	0	0
Improvements 3	0	0	0
Improvements 4	0	0	0
Total Infrastructure Improvements			**2,000**

Building Improvement	Quantity	Price	Total
Improvements 1	1	300	300
Improvements 2	0	0	0
Improvements 3	0	0	0
Improvements 4	0	0	0
Total Infrastructure Improvements			**300**

What is Start-up-cost?

Start-up cost lists all your administrative expenses, from license fees to rent. Sales and marketing are also listed as a part of your start-up-cost. If your business is a new business, then all the associated costs should be listed. It is important to be as realistic as possible when inputting all your costs.

Below is an example of your Start-Up Cost as seen in your A NEW START software.

Start-Up Cost Assumptions

License Fees	Cost of Fees	Advertisment Fees	Cost of Fees
Registration of Business Name	100	Newspaper	250
Business Liscence Fees	50	Radio	500
Other Fees	100	Television	300
Total Fees	250	**Total Fees**	1,050

Incorporation		Promotions	
Incorporation of Business	100	Live Remote	1,200
Legal Fees	1,200	Opening Party	500
Government Fees	300	Other Fees	0
Total Fees	1,600	**Total Fees**	1,700

Utilities Deposits		Signage	
Electricty Deposit	250	Signs	500
Phone Deopsit	250	Billboards	1,000
Water Deposit	150	Web Banners	500
Internet Deposit	50	Other Fees	0
Total Utilties Deposit	700	**Total Fees**	2,000

Insurance		Web Site & logo Design	
Building Insurance	0	Website Design	1,200
Equipment Insurance	250	Logo Design	300
Medical Insurance	350	Other Fees	0
Total Insurance	600	**Total Fees**	1,500

Rent		Marketing Material	
First Month	2,400	Business Cards	450
Security Deposit & Last Month	1,200	Brochures	250
Other fees	0	Magazine Ads	1,000
Total Rent Deposit	3,600	**Total Fees**	1,700

What is a Pro Forma Income Statement?

An income statement is a financial statement that reveals whether a business is profitable.

An income statement, which is also referred to as a profit and loss statement or an operation statement, reveals profit or loss over a specific period. Your A NEW START software has a detailed monthly income statement as well as a 5-year statement.

Below is an example of your 5 Year Income Statement as seen in your A NEW START software.

5 Year Income Statement

	2007	2008	2009	2010	2011
	$	$	$	$	$
Sales Revenue	609,000	669,900	736,890	810,579	891,63
Cost of Sales	142,200	156,420	172,062	189,268	208,19
Gross Margin	**466,800**	**513,480**	**564,828**	**621,311**	**683,44**
Gross Profit Margin %	76.65%	76.65%	76.65%	76.65%	76.65
Operating Expense					
Marketing & Advertising	17,400	18,270	19,184	20,143	21,15
Shipping & freight	3,600	3,780	3,969	4,167	4,37
Management admin staff	24,000	25,200	26,460	27,783	29,17
Salaries/ Wages	36,000	37,800	39,690	41,675	43,75
Legal/ Accounting	0	0	0	0	
Automobile	3,600	3,780	3,969	4,167	4,37
Office Supplies	9,840	10,332	10,849	11,391	11,96
Fixed Expenses					
Rent	14,400	15,120	15,876	16,670	17,50
Utilities	7,380	7,749	8,136	8,543	8,97
Loan Payments Interest	14,888	14,627	14,340	14,022	13,67
National Insurance Rate %	3,240	3,402	3,572	3,751	3,93
Bad debts	609	670	737	811	89
Maintenance & Repairs	2,400	2,520	2,646	2,778	2,91
Depreciation	6,343	6,343	6,343	643	64
Start-up Costs	12,800	0	0	0	
Total Operating Expenses	**156,500**	**149,594**	**155,770**	**156,544**	**163,32**
Earnings before Tax	**310,300**	**363,886**	**409,058**	**464,767**	**520,11**
Taxes	**46,680**	**51,348**	**56,483**	**62,131**	**68,34**
Net Income (Loss)	**263,620**	**312,538**	**352,575**	**402,636**	**451,77**
Operating Profit %	50.95%	54.32%	55.51%	57.34%	58.33

SALES REVENUE

Total number of sales

COST OF SALES

The key to calculating your cost of sales is that you do not overlook any costs that you have incurred. Calculate cost of sales of all products and services used to determine total net sales. Where inventory is involved, do not overlook transportation costs. Also include any direct labor.

GROSS PROFIT

Subtract the total cost of sales from the total net sales to obtain gross profit.

GROSS PROFIT MARGIN

The gross profit is expressed as a percentage of total sales (revenues). It is calculated by dividing gross profits by total net sales.

CONTROLLABLE

(ALSO KNOWN AS VARIABLE) EXPENSES

- Salary expenses - Base pay plus overtime.
- Payroll expenses - Include paid vacations, sick leave, health insurance, unemployment insurance and social security taxes.
- Outside services - Include costs of subcontracts, overflow work and special or one- time services.
- Supplies - Services and items purchased for use in the business.

- Repair and maintenance - Regular maintenance and repair, including periodic large expenditures such as painting.
- Advertising - Include desired sales volume and classified directory advertising expenses.
- Car delivery and travel - include charges if personal car is used in business, including parking, tools, buying trips, etc.
- Accounting and legal - Outside professional services.

FIXED EXPENSES

- Rent - List only real estate used in business.
- Depreciation - Amortization of capital assets.
- Utilities - Water, heat, light, etc.
- Insurance - Fire or liability on property or products.
- Include workers' compensation.
- Loan repayments - Interest on outstanding loans.
- Miscellaneous - Unspecified; small expenditures without separate accounts.

TOTAL EXPENSES

- Net profit (loss)
- Before taxes

TAXES

Net profit (loss) after taxes

Determine the total number of units of products or services you realistically expect to sell each month in each department at the prices you expect to get. Use this step to create the projections to review your pricing practices.

- What returns, allowances and mark-downs can be expected?
- Exclude any revenue that is not strictly related to the business.

Net Profit (loss)

(before taxes) - Subtract total expenses from gross profit.

Taxes - Include inventory and sales tax, excise tax, real estate tax, etc. Net Profit (loss)

(after taxes) - Subtract taxes from net profit (before taxes)

PRO FORMA BALANCE SHEET

The balance sheet will help us to evaluate the liquidity (and solvency) of any company. Liquidity is determined by how quickly, usually within one year, a company can convert its assets into cash, in the event there is the need to pay off outstanding loans. In most instances, the company's balance sheet lists assets in accordance to level of liquidity. Thus, cash is usually listed first followed by property, land, or equipment and so on.

Below is an example of your Balance Sheet as seen in your A NEW START software.

5 Year Balance Sheet

	2007	2008	2009	2010	2011
ASSETS					
Current Assets					
Cash	406,202	721,837	1,077,172	1,476,495	1,924,541
Accts. Receivable	5,583	6,750	8,034	9,446	11,000
Less Allowance	-609	-1,279	-2,016	-2,826	-3,718
Inventories	23,700	26,070	28,677	31,545	34,699
Prepaid Expense	1900	1900	1900	1900	1,900
Total Curr. Assets	**436,775**	**755,278**	**1,113,767**	**1,516,559**	**1,968,422**
Fixed Assets [net]					
Land	35,000	35,000	35,000	35,000	35,000
Buildings, Furniture & Equipment	19,400	19,400	19,400	19,400	19,400
Less Accumulation Depreciation	-6343	-12686	-19030	-19673	-20316
Total Fixed Assets	**48,057**	**41,714**	**35,370**	**34,727**	**34,084**
Total Assets	**484,832**	**796,992**	**1,149,137**	**1,551,287**	**2,002,506**
Liabilities & Equity					
Currrent Liabilities					
Accounts Payable	23,700	26,070	28,677	31,545	34,699
Other loans	0	0	0	0	0
Total Current Liabilities	**23,700**	**26,070**	**28,677**	**31,545**	**34,699**
Bank Debt	147,512	144,764	141,727	138,373	134,667
Total Liabilities	**171,212**	**170,834**	**170,404**	**169,918**	**169,367**
Retained Earnings	263,620	576,158	928,733	1,331,369	1,783,140
Owner Equity	50,000	50,000	50,000	50,000	50,000
Total Equity	313,620	626,158	978,733	1,381,369	1,833,140
Total Liabilities & Equity	**484,832**	**796,992**	**1,149,137**	**1,551,287**	**2,002,506**

ASSETS

List anything of value that is owned or legally due the business. Total assets include all net values. These are the amounts derived when you subtract depreciation and amortization from the original costs of acquiring the assets.

CURRENT ASSETS

- Cash - List cash and resources that can be converted into cash within 12 months of the date of the balance sheet (or during one established cycle of operation). Include money on hand and demand deposits in the bank, e.g., checking accounts and regular savings accounts.

- Petty cash - If your business has a fund for small miscellaneous expenditures, include the total here.

Accounts receivable -The amounts due from customers in payment for merchandise or services.

- Inventory - Includes raw materials on hand, work in progress and all finished goods, either manufactured or purchased for resale.

Short-term investments -Also called temporary investments or marketable securities.

these include interest - or dividend-yielding holdings expected to be converted into cash within a year. List stocks and bonds, certificates of deposit and time-deposit savings accounts at either their cost or market value, whichever is less.

- Prepaid expenses - Goods, benefits or services a business buys or rents in advance.

Examples are office supplies, insurance protection and floor space.

LONG-TERM INVESTMENTS

These are also called long-term assets, these are holdings the business intends to keep for at least a year and that typically yield interest or dividends. Included are stocks, bonds and savings accounts earmarked for special purposes.

FIXED ASSETS

These include called plant and equipment, as well as all resources a business owns or acquires for use in operations and not intended for resale. Fixed assets may be leased. Depending on the leasing arrangements, both the value and the liability of the leased property may need to be listed on the balance sheet.

- Land - List original purchase price without allowances for market value.
- Buildings
- Improvements
- Equipment
- Furniture
- Automobiles/vehicles

CURRENT LIABILITIES

List all debts, monetary obligations and claims payable within 12 months or within one cycle of operation. They typically include the following:

- Accounts payable -
- Amounts owed to suppliers for goods and services purchased in connection with business operations.
- Notes payable -

The balance of principal due to pay off short-term debt for borrowed funds. This also includes the current amount due of the total balance on notes whose terms exceed 12 months.

- Interest payable -

Any accrued fees due for use of both short- and long-term borrowed capital and credit extended to the business.

- Taxes payable -

Amounts estimated by an accountant to have been incurred during the accounting period.

- Payroll accrual - Salaries and wages currently owed.

LONG-TERM LIABILITIES

Notes payable - List notes, contract payments or mortgage payments due over a period exceeding 12 months or one cycle of operation. They are listed by outstanding balance less the current position due.

NET WORTH

Also called owner's equity, net worth is the claim of the owner(s) on the assets of the business. In a proprietorship or partnership, equity is each owner's original investment plus any earnings after withdrawals.

PAID IN CAPITAL

Capital that is brought in by investors in return for stock. It is not capital that is generated through the operation of the company.

Retained Earnings

When profits generated by a company is reinvest back into the business.

TOTAL LIABILITIES AND NET WORTH

The sum of these two amounts must always match that for total assets.

Cash Flow Projection

A cash flow projection is a forecast of the difference between cash coming "in" the business and cash going "out" of the business. Cash flow statements show monthly inflows and outflows of cash. It shows a company's cash status at the end of each month. A cash flow statement provides a glimpse of how much money a business has at any given time and when it is likely to need more cash.

Below is an example of your Cash Flow Statement as seen in your A NEW START software

5 Year Cash Flow

	2007	2008	2009	2010	2011
	$	$	$	$	$
Cash On Hand	0	406,202	721,837	1,077,172	1,476,495
Cash Receipts					
Cash Sales	609,000	669,900	736,890	810,579	891,637
Accounts Recievable	-30,450	-33,495	-36,845	-40,529	-44,582
Collections	24,868	32,328	35,561	39,117	43,028
Cash Injection Loan	200,000	0	0	0	0
Total Cash Inflow	803,418	668,733	735,606	809,167	890,083
Total Cash Available	803,418	668,733	735,606	809,167	890,083
Cash Outflow					
Marketing & Ads.	17,400	18,270	19,184	20,143	21,150
Shipping & freight	3,600	3,780	3,969	4,167	4,376
Management Staff	23,184	24,343	25,560	26,838	28,180
Wages Staff	34,776	36,515	38,341	40,258	42,270
Legal Accounting	0	0	0	0	0
Automobile	3,600	3,780	3,969	4,167	4,376
Inventories	142,200	156,420	172,062	189,268	208,195
Office Supplies	9,840	10,332	10,849	11,391	11,961
Rent	14,400	15,120	15,876	16,670	17,503
Utilities	7,380	7,749	8,136	8,543	8,970
Loan payment	17,376	17,376	17,376	17,376	17,376
National Insurance Rate %	5,280	5,544	5,821	6,112	6,418
Maintenance & Repairs	2,400	2,520	2,646	2,778	2,917
Capital Purchase	54,400	0	0	0	0
Taxes	46,680	51,348	56,483	62,131	68,344
Start Up Cost	14,700	0	0	0	0
Total Cash Outflow	397,216	353,097	380,271	409,843	442,037
Total Cash Flow	206,202	315,636	355,335	399,323	448,046
Owner's Withdrawal	0	0			
Cash Status (end of Year)	406,202	721,837	1,077,172	1,476,495	1,924,541

BREAK-EVEN ANALYSIS

This section shows at which point sales start earning profit for the company. These figures demonstrate the volume of sales, in units, and dollars that must be generated to cover fixed and variable expenses. At the break-even point, you start becoming profitable. Normally this data is presented in a graph format with sales on the x axis and unit sold on the y axis.

The break-even formula:

Fixed Costs

(Revenue per unit - Variable costs per unit)

Fixed costs: Costs that must be paid whether any units are produced. These costs are fixed only over a specified period of time or range of production.

Variable costs: Costs that vary directly with the number of products produced. (Typically: materials, labor used to produce units, percentage of overhead)

EXAMPLE: Fixed cost $22,034/year 10,000-30,000-unit production range
Variable cost $236
materials $26
10,000-30,000-unit production range
Selling Price $833/unit

No of Units to break even $26/year

($9.00/unit-$5.20/unit) 38 units/year
In this example, 38 units must be sold for a price of $833 before the firm will begin to realize a profit.

Break-Even Analysis

Below is an example of your Break-Even Analysis as seen in your A NEW START Software.

Break-Even Analysis

Break-Even Analysis

Break-Even Point	
Average Selling Price	131.82
Variable Cost Per Sale	31
Fixed Expenses Per Month	16,914

MONTHLY BREAK-EVEN VOLUME

Units Break-Even Units(/mth)	167
Sales Break-Even (/mth)	22,067

FINANCIAL RATIOS:

Providing standard financial ratios helps your business plan reader to analyze how well your company will perform compared to other companies within your industry. For existing companies, show the trends over the last 3 to 5 years to outline any improvements in your performance. Ratio analysis helps you evaluate the weak and strong points in your financial and managerial performance.

Ratios:

Gross Margin (Gross Profit = Net Sales - Cost of Goods Sold) This ratio is the percentage of sales dollars left after subtracting the cost of goods sold from net sales. It measures the percentage of sales dollars remaining (after obtaining or manufacturing the goods sold) available to pay the overhead expenses of the company.

Gross Margin Ratio = Gross Profit

Net Sales

Net Profit Margin Ratio: This ratio is the percentage of sales dollars left after subtracting the Cost of Goods sold and all expenses, except income taxes.

It is calculated before income tax because tax rates and tax liabilities vary from company to company.

Net Profit Margin Ratio = Net Profit Before Tax

Net Sales

Return on Equity (ROE):

A measure of a company's profitability calculated as net income divided by equity. ROE shows you what you've earned on your investment in the business during the accounting period. Bankers often refer to this ratio as ROI — return on investment.

Return on Equity = Net Profit

Equity

Return on Investment (ROI): The ROI is perhaps the most important ratio of all. It is the percentage of return on funds invested in the business by its owners.

Return on Investment = Net Profit before Tax

Net Worth

Return on Assets (ROA): These measures how efficiently profits are being generated from the assets employed in the business when compared with the ratios of firms in a similar business.

Return on Assets = Net Profit Before Tax

Total Assets

Current Ratio: The current ratio is one of the best-known measures of financial strength. It is a measure of the cash or near cash position or the liquidity of a firm. The higher the ratio, the more liquid the company, and short-term creditors have some assurance that they will be paid in full.

                         Total Current Assets
Current Ratio =   -------------------------
                         Total Current Liabilities

Quick Ratio: The quick ratio is sometimes called the "acid-test" ratio and is one of the best measures of liquidity. It is a measure of a firm's ability to meet its current obligations.

                         Current asset - Inventory
Quick Ratio =   -------------------------
                         Total Current Liabilities

Debt to equity ratios indicates the company's proportion of liabilities relative to their equity used to finance a company's assets. The higher your debt to equity ratio is, the riskier it is for potential investors. It is important to note that if the ratio is greater than 1, most assets are financed through debt. If it is smaller than 1, assets are primarily financed through equity

Debt/Equity Ratio =   Total Liabilities

Net Worth

Net Worth is defined as total assets minus total liabilities.
Net Worth = Total Assets - Total Liabilities.

Ratios

Below is an example of your five-Year Ratio as seen in your A NEW START Software.

5 Year Ratio Analysis

	2007	2008	2009	2010	2011
Gross Margin	76.65%	76.65%	76.65%	76.65%	76.65%
Net Margin	66.47%	70.87%	72.42%	74.80%	76.10%
Return on Equity	84.06%	49.91%	36.02%	29.15%	24.64%
Return on Investment	64.00%	45.66%	35.60%	29.96%	25.97%
Return on Asset	64.00%	45.66%	35.60%	29.96%	25.97%
Current Ratio	18.43%	28.97%	38.84%	48.08%	56.73%
Quick Ratio	17.43%	27.97%	37.84%	47.08%	55.73%
Debt to equity	0.55%	0.27%	0.17%	0.12%	0.09%
Net Worth	484,832	796,992	1,149,137	1,551,287	2,002,506
Sales/Net Worth	1.94%	1.07%	0.75%	0.59%	0.49%
Net Sale/Assets	1.26%	0.64%	0.49%	0.40%	0.34%
Net Profit/Total Asset	0.54%	0.39%	0.31%	0.26%	0.23%
Net Profit/Net worth	0.54%	0.39%	0.31%	0.26%	0.23%

FINANCIAL ASSUMPTIONS:

Sales Assumptions

These are critical to properly convey the "reasons behind the numbers" for outsiders reviewing your financial projections. Explain how you calculated the numbers you used in your financial statements.

For example, we will sell 20 units per month at $1,500 per unit for a total revenue of $30,000. Your sales assumption in your software uses the weighted average price of all your products or services.

Below is an example of your Sales Assumption as seen in your A NEW START Software.

Sales Forecast Assumptions

Sales Unit Price	Selling Price	Total Units
Software	25	150
Accessories	35	200
PC's	1,200	15
Work Station	1,100	20
Product/Service A	0	0
Total		385

Cost of Sales	Cost Price	Total Unit
Software	5	150
Accessories	8	200
PC's	300	15
Work Station	250	20
Product/Service A	0	0
Total Cost of Sale		385

Sales		
Software	3,750	
Accessories	7,000	
PC's	18,000	
Work Station	22,000	
Product/Service A	0	
Total Monthly Sales	50,750	

Total Cost of Sales		
Software	750	
Accessories	1,600	
PC's	4,500	
Work Station	5,000	
Product/Service A	0	
Total Monthly Cost of Sales	11,850	

Expense

Expenses shows the monthly cost of office and utility supply. Also, it details the cost of your marketing and advertisement.

Expense Assumptions

Office Supplies	
Paper	150
Pens	100
Envelopes	200
Message Pad	50
Note Pad	20
Computer Supplies	300
Total Office Supplies	**820**

Utility & Rent Expense	
Rent	1,200
Light	250
Phone	150
Cable	75
Web Maintenance	50
Water	90
Gas	0
Total Utility & Rent Cost	**1,815**

Other Expense	
Legal & Accounting	0
Maintenance & Repair	200
Automobile Expense	300
Insurance	150
Shipping Expense	300
Total Other Expense	**950**

Marketing & Advertising	
News Paper Ads	250
Television Ads	200
Radio Ads	350
Brochures	150
Travel Expenses	500
Total Marketing & Advertising Cost	**1,450**

Assumption

Your expense assumptions are your operational expenses such as wages, salaries, marketing, insurance and other monthly re-accruing expenses.

Payroll Expenses Assumption

Payroll expense is cost that is associated with your monthly payroll over-head expense. This section includes Staff wages as well as the number of Staff. Your Payroll Assumption includes provision for manager and supervisor wages.

The total monthly wages will be calculated automatically and exported to the Income statement.

Below is an example of your Payroll Expense as seen in your A NEW START Software.

Payroll Expenses Assumptions

Staff Wages	No. Of Staff	Monthly Wage	Total Wages
Sales Agents	3	1,000	3,000
Staff 2	0	0	0
Total Staff Wages			3,000
Management Wages	No. of Mgn Staff	Monthly Wage	Total Wages
Manager	1	2,000	2,000
Supervisior	0	0	0
Total Mgn. Wages			2,000
Total Monthly Payrol Expense			5,000

Inventory Assumptions

List all your start-up inventories as well as office equipment, office furniture and office supplies. You inventory assumption also has provisions for any machinery that will be needed for the operation of your business. It also incurves vehicles, land cost, building cost, construction cost and building improvement cost.

Below is an example of your Inventory Assumptions as seen in your A NEW START Software.

Inventory Assumptions

Inventory1	Quantity	Price	Total
Software	1000	5	5,000
Accessories	50	8	400
PC's	20	500	10,000
Work Station	10	450	4,500
Item 5	0	0	0
Total Inventory 1			**19,900**
Inventory2	QUANTITY	PRICE	TOTAL
Item 1	0	0	0
Item 2	0	0	0
Item 3	0	0	0
Item 4	0	0	0
Total Inventory 2			**0**
Inventory3	Quantity	Price	Total
Item 2	0	0	0
Item 3	0	0	0
Item 4	0	0	0
Total Inventory 3			**0**

General Assumptions

General assumptions are tied to the rest of your business plan and it affect your financials. The assumptions affect your profit and loss, balance sheet, cash flow, ratios, and your 5-year projections.

Below is an example of your General Assumption as seen in your A NEW START Software.

General Assumptions

Annual Growth Rate %	10%
Tax Rate%	15%
National Insurance Rate %	5.4%
Employee Deduction - National Insurance	3.4%
Inflation Rate %	5%
Inventory Turnover (Days)	60
Days of Payment	30
Days of Collection	60
Bad Debt Rate %	2%
Sales on Credit %	5.00%

APPENDIX A

Contract with Clients

If you have contracts that are signed or pending with clients or potential clients, they should also be included in this section of your plan.

Make sure that all your contracts are completed with names, addresses and telephone numbers as well as expiration dates.

All other legal ramifications in your contracts should also be noted in this section as an addendum.

Employment Contracts

All signed employment contracts with potential employees should be included in this section of your plan.

Employee Considerations

This section of your plan should include information about the projected staff for your company. Include the projected salaries, benefits as well as the minimum requirements for employment (i.e. experience). If you have an employee manual that outlines employment guidelines and benefits it should also be included in this section of your plan.

Insurance Considerations

Your employee manual should also include health, life and disability insurance information you intend to offer employees.

Example Design of Job Description

Job Title: President

Job Summary
To provide direction and leadership of short and long-term goals as it relates to their mission of the organization.

Duties
The duties of the president are to ensure the coordination and cohesiveness of the organization as they pertain to the organization's goals.

Time Required
CREATING STRATEGIC OBJECTIVE..................................50%

READING REPORTS TO THE PRESIDENT..........................25%

PLANNING SESSIONS WITH VICE PRESIDENT................25%

Specifications
EDUCATION: Minimum Bachelor's Degree, MBA preferred

EXPERIENCE: Minimum 5 years of executive management experience.

CHAPTER 6

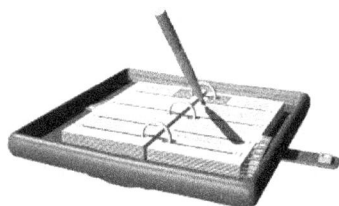

Business Plan Worksheet

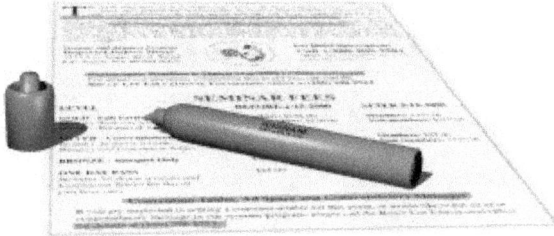

It is time to begin writing your very own Business Plan.
Now that you have completed answering the questions provided above, use the data to fill in the blank spaces in your business plan.

Fill in the blank spaces under the heading and the sub-headings as best as you can. Try to be as thorough and as concise as possible with your answers. This guide will assist you in the structuring of your plan.

Once you have completed this section, you are one step closer to having your very own professional business plan.

_____

_____

_____

DISCLAIMER!

This business plan is the property of _____, Inc. Due to the fact that it contains confidential information proprietary to _____, Inc., no copies may be made whatsoever of the contents herein. Neither can any party not previously authorized, discuss said contents. Officers. This copy must be returned to _____, Inc. upon request.

Executive Summary

_____

_____

_____

_____

Objectives

_____

_____

_____

_____

Mission

_____

_____

_____

_____

Company

_____

_____

_____

Company Ownership

_____

_____

_____

Company History

_____

_____

_____

_____

Product Lines/Services

_____

_____

_____

_____

Location and Facilities

_____

_____

_____

_____

Promotions

_____

_____

_____

_____

Pricing

_____

_____

_____

_____

Cost

_____

_____

_____

Industry Analysis

_____

_____

_____

_____

Market Forecast

_____

_____

_____

_____

Competition

_____

_____

_____

Market Share

_____

_____

_____

Business Strategy

_____

_____

_____

_____

Market Strategy

_____

_____

_____

_____

Market Segment

_____

_____

_____

Distribution Channel

_____

_____

_____

_____

SWOT Analysis

_____

_____

_____

_____

Sales Plan

_____

_____

_____

_____

Business Alliance

_____

_____

_____

Service

_____

_____

_____

_____

Organization

_____

_____

_____

Organizational Structure

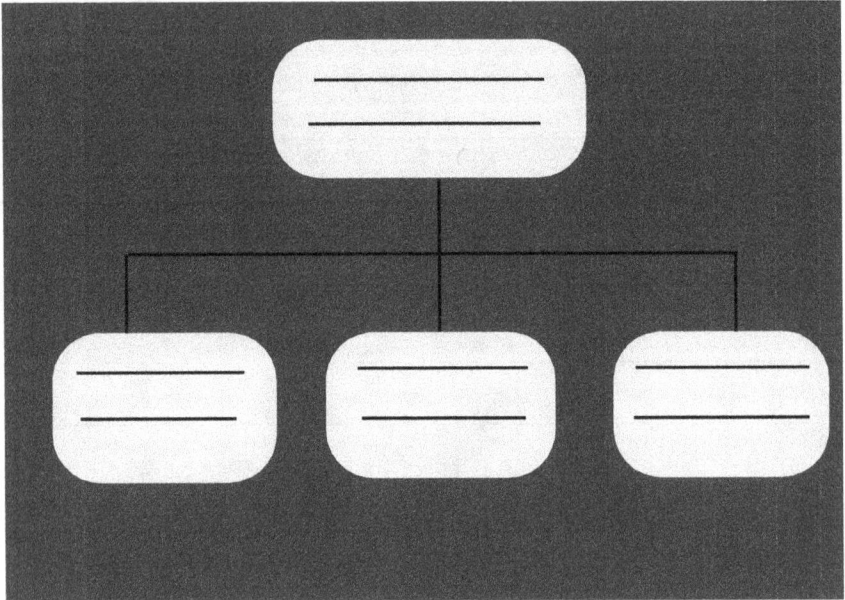

Management Team

Important note:
A resume of all key personnel should be included in this section.

_____

_____

_____

Name, Position

_____

_____

_____

Name, Position

_____

_____

_____

Please note--A job description is needed for each position.

Job Description
Design OF JOB Description
JOB TITLE:

_____

JOB SUMMARY

_____

_____

DUTIES

_____

_____

_____

TIME REQUIRED
CREATING STRATEGIC OBJECTIVES _____%
READING REPORTS TO THE PRESIDENT_____%
PLANNING SESSIONS WITH VICE PRESIDENT_____%

SPECIFICATION
EDUCATION: _____
EXPERIENCE: _____

Management Team Gaps

_____

_____

_____

Other Management Team Considerations

_____

_____

_____

Financial Analysis

_____

_____

_____

_____

Financial Plan

_____

_____

_____

_____

Chapter 6

FINANCIAL ASSUMPTIONS

It is time to work on your financial assumptions.

Completing the text aspect of your plan is only the first of a two part equation. Your financial assumption gives your business plan purpose. It is important that you are as realistic as possible when entering your financial assumptions. You will have to do some research to ensure that your data is accurate.

Bankers and financial analysts don't want to see overly projected forecasts. Inflating your numbers will work against you because it indicates that your plan is not viable. Remember, be as realistic as possible.

Understanding your financial situation is extremely vital. Your financials give you the opportunity to see your business in stages over a long period of time. It also tells you if your business will be a profitable one or whether you will have enough capital to start and sustain your business.

Financial Assumptions

Start-Up Cost Assumptions	
License Fees	**Cost of Fees**
Registration of Business	
Business license Fees	
Other Fees	
Total Fees	
Advertisement	**Cost of Fees**
Newspaper	
Radio	
Newspaper	
Total Fees	
Incorporation	**Cost of Fees**
Incorporation of Business	
Legal Fees	
Government Fees	
Total Fees	
Promotions	**Cost of Fees**
Live Remote	
Opening Party	
Other Fees	
Total Fees	
Utilities Deposits	**Cost of Fees**
Electricity Deposit	
Phone Deposit	
Water Deposit	
Internet Deposit	
Total Utilities Deposit	
Signage	**Cost of Fees**
Signs	
Billboards	
Other Fees	

Other Fees	
Total Fees	
Web Site/ logo Design	
Website Design	
Logo Design	
Other Fees	
Total Fees	
Insurance	
Building Insurance	
Equipment Insurance	
Medical Insurance	
Total Insurance	
Rent	
First Month	
Security Deposit/Last Month	
Other fees	
Total Rent Deposit	
Marketing Material	
Business Cards	
Brochures	
Other Fees	
Total Fees	

Fixed Assets Assumptions			
Furniture & Equipment	**Quantity**	**Price**	**Total**
Total Furniture & Equipment Costs			
Machinery	**Quantity**	**Price**	**Total**

Total Machinery Cost			
Real Estate	**Quantity**	**Price**	**Total**
Total Real Estate Cost			
Infrastructure Improvements	**Quantity**	**Price**	**Total**
Total Infrastructure Improvements			
Building Improvement	**Quantity**	**Price**	**Total**
Total Building Improvements			

Inventory Assumptions			
Inventory 1	**Quantity**	**Price**	**Total**
Total Inventory 1			
Inventory 2	**Quantity**	**Price**	**Total**
Total Inventory 2			
Inventory 3	**Quantity**	**Price**	**Total**
Total Inventory 3			

Payroll Expenses Assumptions			
Staff Wages	No. of Staff	Monthly Wage	Total
Staff 1			
Staff 1			
Total Staff Wages			
Staff Wages	No. of Staff	Monthly Wage	Total
Staff 1			
Staff 1			
Total Staff Wages			

Start-Up Capital	
Start Up Cash	
Owner's Investments	
Total Partner Contribution	
Bank Loan	Total Bank
Total Bank Loan	
Other Loan	Total Bank
Total Other Loan	

Bank Loan	Total Bank Loan
Total Bank Loan	
Other Loan	Total other Loan
Total Other Loan	
Total Capitalization	

Loan Payment Schedule	
Total Amount of Loan	
Loan Payment Schedule	
Enter Values	
Loan Amount	
Annual interest Rate	
Number of Years	
Number of payments per year	

Once you have entered your values, the software is designed to automatically calculate your payment schedule over a 5-year period.

Expense Assumptions	
Office Supplies	**Cost**
Paper	
Pens	
Envelopes	
Message Pad	
Note Pad	
Computer Supplies	
Total Office Supplies	

Utility & Rent Expense	**Cost**
Rent	
Light	
Phone	
Cable	
Web Maintenance	
Water	
Gas	
Total Utility & Rent Cost	

Other Expenses	Cost
Legal & Accounting	
Maintenance & Repair	
Automobile Expense	
Insurance	
Shipping Expense	
Total Other Expenses	
Marketing & Advertising	**Cost**
Newspaper Ads	
Television Ads	
Radio Ads	
Brochures	
Travel Expenses	
Total Marketing & Advertising Costs	

In this section, all your expenses are supposed to be calculated on a monthly basis.

Sales Forecast Assumptions		
Sales Unit Price	Selling Price	Total Units
Total		
Cost of Sales	Selling Price	Total Units
Total		

FINANCIAL ASSUMPTIONS

ANSWERS TO QUESTIONS

1. Entrepreneur

A person who starts and or operates a business.

2. What are the characteristics of an Entrepreneur?

a. Great Imagination
b. Taking-Action
c. Risk-Taking
d. Determination
e. Talents

3. Barriers Facing Entrepreneurs:

a. Cost Associated with starting
b. Long Hours
c. Fear of Failure
d. Physical and Emotional Stress
e. Personal Resistance
f. Fear of the Unknown
g. Fear of risks
h. Lack of confidence to tackle the venture
i. Resistance to the venture itself
j. Lack of resources

k. Competition

l. Lack of Support in providing Start-up funds (Government, Banks, Investors etc...)

m. Resistance to change

n. Fear about new Ideas

o. Negative influences

4. Twelve Steps in Developing a Business

1) Identifying the opportunity (what)

2) Identifying the need for a product

3) Researching & analyzing

4) the opportunity (For what purpose)

5) Researching the market

6) Identifying the business (How)

7) Deciding on a business Venture

8) Planning the Business (Business Plan)

9) Who, What, When & How

10) Developing the business

11) Raising Funds, Allocate Tasks, Take Action

12) Monitoring & Evaluating Process

13) Checking on progress, Adjusting plan as necessary

5. Factors Affecting the Entrepreneur:

a. Human

b. Material

c. Culture

d. Location

6. The four Ps in marketing

1) Product
2) Place
3) Promotion
4) Price

7. What is SWOT Analysis?

1) Strengths
2) Weaknesses
3) Opportunities
4) Threats

Additional Notes

_____

_____

_____

_____

_____

_____

_____

_____

_____

_____

_____

_____

_____

_____

_____

_____

_____

_____

CHAPTER 7

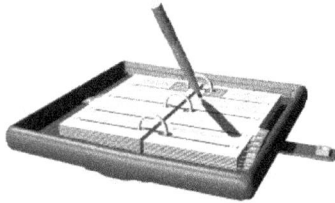

"In all realms of life it takes courage to stretch your limits, express your power, and fulfill your potential. it's no different in the financial realm."

– Suze Orman

Small Business Directory Assistance

United States
Small Business Association
SBA Answer Desk
1-800-U-ASK-SBA (1-800-827-5722)
Send e-mails to: answerdesk@sba.gov
Answer Desk TTY: (704) 344-6640
www.sba.gov/

Business.gov
The official business link to the U.S Government
www.business.gov/

SCORE "Counselors to America's Small Business"
SCORE Association
409 3rd Street, SW, 6th Floor Washington, D.C. 20024

1175 Herndon Pkwy., Suite 900, Herndon, VA 20170
Phone 1-800/634-0245 or 703/487-3612 Fax: 703/487-3066
www.score.org.

U.S. Chamber of Commerce
1615 H Street, NW Washington, DC 20062-2000
Main Number: 202-659-6000
Customer Service: 1-800-638-6582 www.uschamber.com

U.S. Patent and Trademark Office
Mail Stop USPTO Contact Center (UCC)
P.O. Box 1450
Alexandria, VA 22313-1450
Phone: 800-786-9199 or 571-272-1000
Fax: 571-273-3245
E-mail: usptoinfo@uspto.gov www.uspto.gov

U.S. Department of Commerce
1401 Constitution Ave., NW Washington, DC 20230
Phone (202) 482-2000
E-mail Webmaster@doc.gov
www.commerce.gov

United Kingdom
The Department for Business, Enterprise & Regulatory Reform
Ministerial Correspondence Unit
Department for Business, Enterprise & Regulatory Reform
1 Victoria Street
London SW1H 0ET   Call us on 020 7215 5000
Fax us on 020 7215 0105
www.dti.gov.uk

Small Business Support
18 Hertford Street Coventry
Warwickshire CV1 1LF
T: 0870 777 6990
F: 0870 777 6991
info@sbsonline.co.uk www.sbsonline.co.uk

The British Chambers of Commerce
65 Petty France London
SW1H 9EU
Tel: +44 (0)20 7654 5800
Fax: +44 (0)20 7654 5819
Email: info@britishchambers.org.uk
www.chamberonline.co.uk

Bizhelp
ROK Connect Limited Trading as:
BizHelp24 Hallam Business Centre Dronfield
Derbyshire S18 1LS
Web: http://www.bizhelp24.com

International Franchise Association
222 International Drive, Suite 195 B
Portsmouth, NH 03801 USA
Telephone: (+1) 877-808-5295
Fax: (+1) 603-570-2950
Email info@franchise.com
www.franchise.com

The Bahamas
The Bahamas Chamber of Commerce
Shirley Street & Collins Avenue
P. O. Box: N-665
Nassau, Bahamas Tel:(242) 322-2145
Fax:(242) 322-4649

Bahamas Development Bank
Cable Beach, West Bay Street
P. O. Box N-3034
Nassau, Bahamas T: 242 327-5780-6
F: 242 327-5047
info@bahamasdevelopmentbank.com
www.bahamasdevelopmentbank.com

Bahamas Entrepreneurial Venture Fund
28 Cumberland Hill Street
P.O. Box N 1991
Nassau, Bahamas Phone: 356-4114
Fax: 356-4125
www.bahamasventurefund.com

Bahamas Agricultural & Industrial Corporation
Levy Building, East Bay Street PO Box 4940, Nassau, Bahamas
tel: 242-322-3740
fax: 242-322-2133
Email baic@bahamas.net.bs www.bahamasb2b.com/baic

Caribbean
The Barbados Chamber of Commerce and Industry 1st Floor Nemwil House,
Collymore Rock, St. Michael, Barbados, WI.
Website: http//www.bdscham.com

Caribbean American Chamber of Commerce & Industry, Inc.
63 Flushing Ave.
Brooklyn Navy Yard – Building # 5,
Mezzanine A Brooklyn, New York 11205
Tel: (718) 834-4544
Fax: (718) 834-9774
Email: rahastick@msn.com

Caribbean Development Bank
P.O. Box 408
Wildey,St. Michael Barbados, W.I.
Tel. No. (246)431-1600
Fax No. (246)426-7269
Email: info@caribank.org
www.caribank.org/

Caribbean Export Development Agency
Barbados Headquarters: Hastings, Christ Church, Barbados
Mailing: P.O. Box 34B, BARBADOS, W.I.
Tel: (246) 436-0578
Fax: (246) 436-9999
e-mail: info@carib-export.com
www.carib-export.com

Trinidad & Tobago Chamber of Industry & Commerce
Columbus Circle Westmoorings P.O. Box 499
Port of Spain, Trinidad & Tobago W.I. Tel: 868 637 6966
Fax: 868 637 7425
E-mail: chamber@chamber.org.tt
Website: www.chamber.org.tt

Employment Application Form Sample

Please print and fill out all sections
Applicant Information

Name: (last) _____

(first) (M.I) _____

Phone:(Home) _____

(Work) _____

(Cell) _____

Email: _____

Current Address:

Number and street _____

City _____

State & Zip _____

Employment Positions

Position(s) applying for: _____

What days and hours are you available for work? _____

Can you work on the weekends? [ ] Y or [ ] N

Can you work evenings? [ ] Y or [ ] N

Are you available to work overtime? [ ] Y or [ ] N

If hired, on what date can you start working? ____/____/____

Salary desired: $ _____

Personal Information:

Have you ever applied to / worked for this Company before?
[ ] Y or [ ] N

If yes, please explain (include date):

_____

_____

If hired, are you willing to submit to a controlled substance test?
[ ] Y or [ ] N *(failure to pass such a test would prohibit hiring).

Have you ever been convicted of a criminal offense (felony or misdemeanor)? [ ] Y or [ ] N
If yes, please describe the crime - state nature of the crime(s), when and where convicted and disposition of the case.

_____

_____

Education, Training and Experience
High School:

School name: _____

School address: _____

School city, state, zip: _____

Number of years completed: _____

Did you graduate? [ ] Y or [ ] N

Degree / diploma earned: _____

College / University:

School name: _____

School address:_____

School city, state, zip:_____

Number of years completed: _____
Did you graduate? [ ] Y or [ ] N

Degree / diploma earned: _____

Vocational School:

School name: _____

School address: _____

School city, state, zip: _____

Number of years completed: _____
Did you graduate? [ ] Y or [ ] N

Degree / diploma earned: _____

Do you speak, write or understand any foreign languages?
[ ] Y or [ ] N
If yes, describe which languages(s) and how fluent of a speaker you consider yourself to be.

Do you have any other experience, training, qualifications, or skills which you feel should be brought to our attention, in the case that they make you especially suited for working with us? [ ] Y or [ ] N
If yes, please explain?

Employment History

Are you currently employed? [ ] Y or [ ] N

If you are currently employed, may we contact your current employer? [ ] Y or [ ] N

Below, please describe past and present employment positions, dating back five years.

Name of Employer:_____

Name of Supervisor:_____

Telephone Number:_____

Business Type: _____

Address: _____

City, state, zip:_____

Length of Employment (Include Dates): _____

Position & Duties:_____

Reason for Leaving: _____

May we contact this employer for references? [ ] Y or [ ] N

Name of Employer:_____

Name of Supervisor:_____

Telephone Number:_____

Business Type: _____

Address: _____

City, state, zip:_____

Length of Employment (Include Dates): _____

Position & Duties:_____

Reason for Leaving: _____

May we contact this employer for references? [ ] Y or [ ] N

Name of Employer:_____

Name of Supervisor:_____

Telephone Number:_____

Business Type: _____

Address: _____

City, state, zip:_____

Length of Employment (Include Dates): _____

Position & Duties:_____

Reason for Leaving: _____

May we contact this employer for references? [ ] Y or [ ] N

Name of Employer:_____

Name of Supervisor:_____

Telephone Number:_____

Business Type: _____

Address: _____

City, state, zip:_____

Length of Employment (Include Dates): _____

Position & Duties:_____

Reason for Leaving: _____

May we contact this employer for references? [ ] Y or [ ] N

Name of Employer:_____

Name of Supervisor:_____

Telephone Number:_____

Business Type: _____

Address: _____

City, state, zip:_____

Length of Employment (Include Dates): _____

Position & Duties:_____

Reason for Leaving: _____

May we contact this employer for references? [ ] Y or [ ] N

References

List below three persons who have knowledge of your work performance within the last year.

Please include professional references only.

Name - First, Last: _____

Telephone Number: _____

Address: _____

City, state, zip: _____

Occupation: _____

Number of Years Acquainted: _____

Please read and initial each paragraph, then sign below.

    I certify that I have not purposely withheld any information that might adversely affect my chances for hiring. I attest to the fact that the answers given by me are true and correct to the best of my knowledge and ability. I understand that any omission (including any misstatement) of material fact on this application or on any document used to secure can be grounds for rejection of application or, if I am employed by this company, terms for my immediate expulsion from the company. _____

    I permit the company to examine my references, record of employment, education record, and any other information I have provided. I authorize the references I have listed to disclose any information related to my work record and my professional experiences with them, without giving me prior notice of such disclosure. In addition, I release the company, my former employers & all other persons, corporations, partnerships & associations from any & all claims, demands or liabilities arising out of or in any way related to such examination or revelation. _____

Applicant's Signature: _____

Date: _____

Chapter 7

GLOSSARY

ACCOUNTS PAYABLE
Money owed by your business such as bills from suppliers.

ACCOUNTS RECEIVABLE
Money owed to your business such as money owed by customers to whom you have sold goods on credit.

ACCOUNTS RECEIVABLE TURNOVER
The ratio of net credit sales to average account receivable: a measure of how quickly customers pay their bills.

ADVERTISEMENT
A paid public announcement appearing in the media.

AMORTIZATION
A loan is amortized when the total monthly payment is the same each month, but the amount that is applied to principal and interest changes. In the beginning of the loan, most of the monthly payment is applied to **Loan Interest** with only a small amount applied to pay the **Loan Principal.** In the later stages of the loan, most of the payment is applied to the principal balance. A house mortgage is a common example of an amortized loan.

APPRECIATION
Increase in value of property such as land.; opposite to depreciation

ASSET
Any item of value (including cash) owned by your business.

AVAILABLE CREDIT
The amount of open but unused lines of credit. Too much available credit can negatively impact a person's **Credit Score.**

BALANCE SHEET
A financial statement that shows the value of your business at a particular point in time. The Balance Sheet consists of two columns, **Assets** and **Liabilities,** which must be equal.

BOOK VALUE
The original purchase price of a **Capital Expenditure** minus accumulated **Depreciation. Long Term Assets** are listed on a **Balance Sheet** at Book Value.

BREAK-EVEN POINT
The level of sales whereby you are neither making a profit nor incurring a loss. **Revenue** exactly matches **Total Costs** at the Break-Even Point.

BROCHURE
A folded leaflet with an advertising or promotional message.

BUSINESS PLAN
A comprehensive planning document which clearly describes the business developmental objective of an existing or proposed

business. The plan out-lines what, how and from where the resources are needed. It is also a written review of the business to identify strengths and weaknesses, locate needs, and begin planning how to best accomplish the business' objectives.

CAPITAL
The financial investment required to initiate and/or operate an enterprise.

CAPITAL ASSET
An asset that is purchased for long-term use such as machinery and equipment.

CAPITAL EXPENDITURE
An expenditure for an item for use in your business that you expect to use for a long time (more than one year) such as machinery or a vehicle. Capital Expenditures are **Fixed Assets** and are usually subject to **Depreciation.**

CAPITALIZATION
How you are going to raise money for your business.

CASH FLOW PROJECTION
A chart showing the flow of cash into and out of your business on a monthly basis. Also known as a **Cash Flow Statement.**

COMMON STOCK
A class of stock issued by a corporation. It is the most frequently issued type of stock. It carries with it a voting right, however is secondary in priority to preferred stock in dividend and liquidation rights.

CONSUMER
A private individual at whom advertisements are aimed; a buyer.

CONSUMER MARKET
A defined group of consumers.

CORPORATION
A separate and distinct legal entity that acts for, or on behalf of a group of people. A corporation is created by or under the authority of the laws of a state or nation. A corporation may be formed for profit or not for profit.

COST OF GOOD SOLD; COGS:
The amount determined by subtracting the value of the ending merchandise inventory from the sum of the beginning merchandise inventory and the net purchases for the fiscal period.

CURRENT ASSETS
Assets owned by your business that you expect to use within one year such as cash, **Accounts Receivable, Inventory,** or **Raw Materials.**

CURRENT LIABILITIES
Money owed by your business that must be paid within one year such as **Accounts Payable** and **Loan Principal** and **Loan Interest** that is due within one year.

CURRENT RATIO
Current Assets divided by **Current Liabilities.** The Current Ratio measures your business' ability to meet obligations that are coming due soon, such as payments to suppliers or taxes. It is

particularly useful as an early warning signal of an impending cash crisis.

DEBT TO ASSETS RATIO
Total Liabilities divided by **Total Assets.** The Debt to Assets Ratio is a measure of the riskiness of your business. For example, a Debt to Assets Ratio of 75% would indicate that most of the money in your business came from creditors and that your business may have trouble paying a new loan.

DEPRECIATION
Depreciation is a method of accounting for the cost of a **Fixed Asset** over time. Yearly depreciation is included on the Income Statement as an **Operating Expense** and Fixed Assets are shown on the **Balance Sheet** at their original purchase price minus the total amount of Depreciation that has accumulated since the item was purchased. (Land is never depreciated.) Depreciation is a Fixed Cost.

DIRECT COSTS
Costs to your business that are directly related to production and which change with the level of sales; such as costs for **Raw Materials** (for a manufacturer) or **Inventory** bought for resale (for a retailer) This is also known as **Variable Costs.**

ENDING BALANCE
On a **Cash Flow Statement**, the amount of cash left over at the end of the month after all cash outflows have been subtracted from the total inflow of cash. The Ending Balance always equals the **Opening Balance** of the next month.

ENTREPRENEUR
One who takes on the financial risk of the initiation, operation and management of a business.

EQUITY
The value of the owner's investment in the business. On the **Balance Sheet**, Equity is calculated by subtracting **Total Assets** from **Total Liabilities** and is written on the liability side of the Balance Sheet.

EQUITY INVESTOR
A person who invests money in a business and in return receives part ownership of the business. An equity Investor would be compensated in the form of dividends and/or when he later sells his ownership stake at a profit.

FIXED ASSETS
Items owned by the business that the business expects to use for more than one year such as machinery or vehicles. Also known as **Long Term Assets.**

GROSS MARGIN
Net sales minus cost of goods sold.

GROSS MARGIN PERCENTAGE
The gross margin from an income statement divided by net sales revenue.

GROSS PROFIT
Revenue minus the cost of raw materials used to manufacture the items that were sold (if you are a manufacturer) or Revenue minus

the cost of buying items for re-sale (if you are a retailer). Gross Profit is calculated for each individual item sold and for the business as a whole. Also known as **Cost of Goods Sold.**

INCOME FROM OPERATIONS
Gross profit minus operating expenses such as labor, rent, utilities, etc.

INCOME STATEMENT
A financial statement that measures the profitability of a business. This is also known as the **Profit and Loss Statement** or the **Operating Statement.**

INFLATION
A general rise in the level of prices.

INVENTORY
Items owned by the business for resale.

LIABILITY
Money owed by the business such as **Accounts Payable, Loan Interest,** or **Loan Principal.**

LIMITED LIABILITY COMPANY
A business formed by one or more members. The owners are the members of the company and manage the company unless otherwise stated by the Articles of Organization. A manager means a person or persons designated by the members to manage the limited liability company as provided in the Articles of Organization or an Operating Agreement.

LIMITED PARTNERSHIP

A type of partnership comprised of one or more general partners who manage the business and who are personally liable for partnership debts, and one or more limited partners who contribute capital and share in profits but who take no part in running the business and incur no liability with respect to partnership obligations beyond contribution.

LIQUIDITY

A business that can easilymeet its short-term obligations is said to be liquid. **Current Ratio** is a measure of liquidity.

LOAN INTEREST

The expense of borrowing money. A total loan payment would consist of Loan Interest plus the repayment of Loan Principal.

LOAN PRINCIPAL

The original amount of money borrowed.

LONG TERM LIABILITIES

Money owed by the business that will not be repaid until after at least one year such as the portion of **Loan Principal** that is not due for at least a year.

MANAGEMENT

Those policy makers, planners, and administrators responsible for running a business.

MARKET

The prospective customers for a given product or service.

MARKET SEGMENTATION

The process of dividing a heterogeneous market into several homogeneous sub-markets.

MARKET SHARE

The percentage of the total sales (from all sources) of a service or product represented by the sales made by your enterprise. i.e. your sales divided by total sales

NET INCOME

The difference between your business' total revenues and its total expenses. This caption and amount are usually found at the bottom of a company's Income Statement (also known as "The Bottom Line").

NET OPERATING LOSS

A net operating loss results when business expenses exceed business income for the operating period.

NET PROFIT

Gross Profit minus **Operating Expenses.**

NET PROFIT MARGIN

Net Profit divided by **Revenue.**

NET WORTH

Property owned (assets), minus debts and obligations owed (liabilities), is the owner's equity (net worth).

OPENING BALANCE

On a **Cash Flow Statement**, the amount of cash on-hand at the start of each month before any sales have occurred or any other inflow of cash. The Opening Balance is always equal to the previous month's **Ending Balance.**

OPERATING EXPENSES

Expenses incurred by the business that are not directly related to production such as utilities, salaries, office supplies, etc. Operating Expenses do not change when the business' level of production rises or falls. This is also known as **Overhead, Fixed Costs,** or **Indirect Costs**.

OWNER EQUITY

The difference, if any, between Total Assets and Total Liabilities on a Balance sheet. If assets are more than liabilities, the owner has that amount of equity it the business.

PARTNERSHIP

A legal business relationship of two or more people who share responsibilities, resources, profits, and liabilities.

PREPAID EXPENSES

Amounts paid in advance to a creditor or vendor for goods or services. Insurance premiums are a good example. Prepaid Expenses are a current asset because you paid for goods or services you have not yet received.

PROFIT BEFORE TAXES

is operating profit minus all other expenses (net).

PROPRIETORSHIP

A business owned by one person.

QUICK RATIO

The sum of **Current Assets** minus **Inventory** divided by **Current Liabilities.** The Quick Ratio measures a business' ability to raise money quickly.

RAW MATERIAL

A basic material that becomes part of a physical product; usually comes from mines, forests, oceans, or recycled solid wastes.

RETAINED EARNINGS

Profit made by the business that has not been paid out to the owners as **Dividends.** Retained Earnings are available for reinvestment into the business. On the balance Sheet, Retained Earnings is listed as a **Liability.**

RETURN Of INVESTMENT (ROI)

Profit divided by **Total Assets.** ROI measures how much the business' owner has earned on his/her investment in the business.

REVENUE

Sales (in units) multiplied by price per unit

SOLE PROPRIETORSHIP

A business, usually unincorporated, owned and controlled exclusively by one person.

START-UP COSTS

Expenses incurred before the business opens.

TOTAL ASSETS

Long-Term Assets plus **Current Assets.** The total sum of all property owned by the business including permanent assets such as buildings, machinery, etc.

TOTAL COSTS

Fixed Costs plus **Direct Costs,** Total Liabilities, **Current Liabilities, Long Term Liabilities and Total Liabilities:** The total sum of all money owed by the business (Current Liabilities plus Long Term Liabilities)

TOTAL LIABILITIES

Is the sum of all liability items.

VARIABLE COSTS

Variable expenses that vary directly with the changes in the volume of sales or production, e.g., raw material costs and sales commissions.

WORKING CAPITAL

Current Assets minus **Current Liabilities.** A company has a working capital shortage when it is unable to pay its suppliers and creditors easily and service new orders.

REFERENCES

Chapter 1

LeeAnn E. Moss, Rosanne S. Groves, and Thomas L. Sporleder. (2006) *"Business Plan Assistance on the Web"*. from http://aede.ag.ohio-state.edu/resources/docs/pdf/51CEB60B-9F0F-11D5-ABF300C00D014775.pdf

Lao-tzu "A journey of a thousand miles begins with a single step." Tim Berry." *The Plan-as-You-Go Business Plan." (2007). From http://www.entrepreneur.com/startingabuness/ businessplans/business-plancoachtimberry/article189514.html*

"The Inventions of Thomas Edison' (2007). from http://inventors.about.com/library/inventors/bledison.htm

Anonymous. *"Some men dream of worthy accomplishments, while others stay awake and do them." (2007). From http://www.lilesnet.com/inspiration/dreams.htm*

The Bible. *"A man's gift makes room for him"*. Proverbs 18:16.

General Douglas McArthur." The greatest risk in life is not taking one." (2007) from http://www.educationask.com/quotations/535-Quotations.html

Cox, Josie. *Google is now the world's most valuable brand.* February 1, 2017. https://www.independent.co.uk/news/ business/news/worlds-most-valuable-brands-facebook-google-apple-amazon-a7556571.html.

Dogtiev, Artyom. *App Revenues (2017)*. 2017.
www.businessofapp.com/dada/app-revenues/.

Golmack, Stacy. *Current Trends and Futuer Prospects of The Mobile App Market*. February 20, 2017.
https://www.smashingmagazine.com/2017/02/current-trends-future-prospects-mobile-app-market/.

Louis Antoine Fauvelet de Bourrienne. "Memoirs of Napoleon Bonaparte." (2007). from http://books.google.bs/books

Unknown. *'You cannot discover new oceans, unless you have the courage to lose site of the shore." (2006)* from.
http://www.thinkpowerthoughts.com/page4.html

Chapter 2

Pearlson, K. E., & Saunders, C. S., (2006). Managing & using information systems: A Strategic approach (3rd ed.). Hoboken, NJ: John Wiley & Son, Inc.

Cemerspan. What is the Internet. (2007). from.
http://www.centerspan.org/tutorial/net.htm

Siems, Thomas F.; Ratner, Adam S, *Strengthening Globalization's Invisible Hand*: What Matters Most? Business Economics Source:Business Economics v. 41 no. 4 (October 2006) p. 16-28

Brandyberry, G. *How to survive in a global economy* [Insightful analysis of F. Ghadar's book, Global Tectonics, *What Every Business)needs to Know*]. Purchasing v. 135 no. 16 (November 2 2006) p. 53

Mike Holmes, *Lack of knowledge hastens small business failures (2007)*
ECONOMY, BUSINESS & FINANCE; Pg. 1

Chapter 3

Noe, Hollenbeck, Gerhart, Wright. Human Resource Management," *gaining a competitive advantage*", 6 Eddition, (April 2008) P. 84

Johnson & Weinstein, Superior Customer Value in The New Economy:Concepts and cases, 2nd ed. (April 2008) P.23, CRC Press LLC.

E. Jeromelimiting McCarthy. The Four Ps of Marketing. Carole Hedden, The Product Life Cycle (S Curve)

Maddox, Kate, Adopts New Definition of Marketing (2008), www.marketingpower.com/content24159.php

Michael Porter theory of "differentiation

Drucker, P (1973) Management, Task, Responsibilities, Practices, New York: Harper & Row, 64-65.

NetMBA (The Product Life Cycle) www.netmba.com

5. U.S. Small Business Administration (SBA) Financial description. 6. E-commerce. www.advancedmanufacturing.com 7. Morebusiness.com, Advantages of Incorporating, Copyright 1999 by The Company Corporation. All Rights Reserved 8. Investing For Beginners, Joshua Kennon Albert Humphrey SWAT.

Chapter 4

T Richard Dealtry, 1992 Dynamic SWOT Analysis, Birmingham

www.ingramcontent.com/pod-product-compliance
Lightning Source LLC
Chambersburg PA
CBHW061217220326
41599CB00025B/4673